Cambridge Elements ≡

Elements in Politics and Society in Southeast Asia
edited by
Edward Aspinall
Australian National University
Meredith L. Weiss
University at Albany, SUNY

THE MEANING OF DEMOCRACY IN SOUTHEAST ASIA

Liberalism, Egalitarianism and Participation

Diego Fossati
City University of Hong Kong

Ferran Martinez i Coma
Griffith University

CAMBRIDGE
UNIVERSITY PRESS

Shaftesbury Road, Cambridge CB2 8EA, United Kingdom

One Liberty Plaza, 20th Floor, New York, NY 10006, USA

477 Williamstown Road, Port Melbourne, VIC 3207, Australia

314–321, 3rd Floor, Plot 3, Splendor Forum, Jasola District Centre, New Delhi – 110025, India

103 Penang Road, #05–06/07, Visioncrest Commercial, Singapore 238467

Cambridge University Press is part of Cambridge University Press & Assessment, a department of the University of Cambridge.

We share the University's mission to contribute to society through the pursuit of education, learning and research at the highest international levels of excellence.

www.cambridge.org
Information on this title: www.cambridge.org/9781108977661

DOI: 10.1017/9781108973434

First published 2023

A catalogue record for this publication is available from the British Library.

ISBN 978-1-108-97766-1 Paperback
ISSN 2515-2998 (online)
ISSN 2515-298X (print)

The Meaning of Democracy in Southeast Asia

Liberalism, Egalitarianism and Participation

Elements in Politics and Society in Southeast Asia

DOI: 10.1017/9781108973434
First published online: January 2023

Diego Fossati
City University of Hong Kong

Ferran Martinez i Coma
Griffith University

Author for correspondence: Diego Fossati, dfossati@cityu.edu.hk

Abstract: This Element contributes to existing research with an analysis of public understandings of democracy based on original surveys fielded in Indonesia, Malaysia, the Philippines, Singapore and Thailand. It conceptualizes democracy as consisting of liberal, egalitarian and participatory ideals, and investigates the structure of public understandings of democracy in the five countries. It then proceeds to identify important relationships between conceptions of democracy and other attitudes, such as satisfaction with democracy, support for democracy, trust in institutions, policy preferences and political behaviour. The findings suggest that a comprehensive analysis of understandings of democracy is essential to understand political attitudes and behaviours.

Keywords: public opinion, democratic attitudes, legitimacy, participation, Southeast Asia

ISBNs: 9781108977661 (PB), 9781108973434 (OC)
ISSNs: 2515-2998 (online), 2515-298X (print)

Contents

Further online supplementary material can be accessed
at www.cambridge.org/Fossati_appendix

1 Introduction

Democracy is an appealing normative ideal, and a vast literature has identified high levels of support for democracy worldwide. According to international public opinion surveys, large majorities of respondents anywhere will agree that 'Despite its drawbacks, democracy is the best form of government' or evaluate having a democratic system of government as 'fairly good' or 'very good' (Inglehart, 2003). These figures, however, should not be interpreted as suggesting that high levels of popular demand for democracy exist in most world regions. On the one hand, extremely high levels of support for democracy are observed in societies where liberal values are known to be poorly consolidated, such as in the Middle East (Tessler et al., 2012) or China (Wang, 2007). On the other hand, there is also increasing evidence that ordinary people may either misunderstand what democracy means or may otherwise be unable to articulate a coherent idea of democracy. In their study of democratic misconceptions around the world, for instance, Kirsch and Welzel (2019) find that stated support for democracy is often coupled with authoritarian preferences such as support for unconstrained rule by political, religious or military elites.[1] Furthermore, citizens may erroneously describe as democracies countries that in fact have authoritarian political regimes (Baniamin, 2020), or they may fail to differentiate between democratic and authoritarian features of political regimes (Shin & Kim, 2018).

This research indicates that the idea of democracy is as controversial as it is aspirational. While most will agree that free and fair elections are an essential prerequisite of democracy, what democracy should entail beyond this basic requirement has been the subject of a long-standing normative debate, which has important reverberations for how democracy should be measured and assessed. Just to mention some of the main conceptualizations, for many scholars a democracy is also supposed to be *liberal*, meaning a political regime that limits the power of electoral majorities with checks and balances to protect individual and minority rights (Fawcett, 2018). Others have articulated a *participatory* notion of democracy, stressing the importance of citizen involvement in democratic politics beyond the formal channels provided by delegation to elected representatives (Barber, 2003). Yet others have emphasized the importance of an *egalitarian* or *social* conception of democracy, which acknowledges the importance of material and immaterial inequalities and asks whether all citizens are equally empowered to participate in and benefit from democratic politics (Young, 2002).

---

[1] See also Schedler and Sarsfield's (2007) study, 'Democrats with adjectives: Linking direct and indirect measures of democratic support'.

Such conceptual distinctions are important for democratic practice. Given that, as we further discuss later in this Element, support for democracy is key for regime legitimacy and democratic consolidation, understanding what exactly citizens mean by 'democracy' is a fundamental endeavour for research into democracy. Existing studies have leveraged the increasing availability and reach of international public opinion research programmes to analyse how conceptions of democracy vary across country and region. Some of this research has analysed open-ended questions to study what citizens mean by 'democracy', and it has generally found that, in most nations, democracy is identified not only with electoral procedures, but also with basic freedoms and civil liberties (Dalton et al., 2007). Although this would suggest that liberal understandings of democracy are prevalent in most world regions, studies based on more structured, closed-ended questions have yielded different results.

International survey research programmes such as the World Values Survey, the European Social Survey and the regionally based Global Barometer surveys include various questions to study popular understandings of democracy. Several studies have analysed these and other data sets, especially by studying variation in conceptions of democracy across regions (Dalton et al., 2007; Norris, 2011) or across countries within specific regions – such as Europe (Ferrín & Kriesi, 2016), Asia (Chu & Huang, 2010; Robbins, 2015), Africa (Letsa & Wilfahrt, 2018; Mattes & Bratton, 2007) or Latin America (Camp, 2001) – but also by analysing differences among social groups (Ceka & Magalhaes, 2020) or between political elites and ordinary citizens (Aspinall et al., 2020). As a recent review summarizes (Shin & Kim, 2018), these studies have demonstrated that citizens in any world region have a complex, multidimensional understanding of democracy. Although most of them will identify freedoms and rights as a key feature of democratic governance, ordinary people do not typically view liberal freedoms as the sole – or even the main – dimension of democracy.

Research on Southeast Asia, the empirical focus of this Element, has primarily addressed the question of whether, and to what extent, 'liberal values' are entrenched in the region's political culture. Authoritarian elites have long dominated the political landscape in this region, where economic and social modernizations have not produced consolidated liberal democracies such as those observed in the West (Reilly, 2017). Many scholars have provided nuanced accounts of the predominance of non-liberal ideologies in the region, the unique development of liberal political thought and the fraught relationship between liberalism and democracy (Bourchier, 2014; Chua, 1997; Connors, 2016; David & Holliday, 2018; Thompson, 2021). The overall picture emerging

Table 1 Prioritized dimensions of democracy in Southeast Asia
(Asian Barometer)

Country	Social equality	Good governance	Procedures	Freedom and liberty
The Philippines	29%	21%	22%	28%
Thailand	36%	33%	17%	13%
Cambodia	27%	24%	27%	22%
Indonesia	26%	34%	23%	17%
Singapore	30%	36%	18%	16%
Malaysia	25%	25%	26%	14%
Vietnam	42%	35%	17%	6%

Note: The percentages represent the share of responses prioritizing each dimension in various countries. Data from Asia Barometer, third wave 2010–12. From Huang (2017).

from this literature is one of a region where a strong liberal culture is missing and democracy is rarely understood as a set of inalienable individual rights and constraints to executive power.

Empirical, survey-based research on public opinion in Southeast Asia has corroborated these qualitative insights. This work is mostly based on data from the Asian Barometer survey, which includes a series of multiple-choice questions that ask respondents to select the most important feature of democracy from among four choices, which can be traced back to two main dimensions: one 'procedural' (a mix of electoral and liberal elements) and one 'substantive' (a mix of socio-economic equality and 'good governance'). In various articles and book chapters (Chu & Huang, 2010; Huang et al., 2013), analyses based on these data have consistently shown that substantive understandings of democracy trump liberal and electoral conceptions,[2] and these findings have been confirmed in studies based on other data sources (Dore et al., 2014, p. 34). As shown in Table 1, although there are important differences across countries, most Southeast Asian citizens appear to understand democracy in terms of policy outcomes (i.e., social equality and good governance), rather than liberal checks and balances or specific features of electoral politics.[3]

---

[2] But see also Chu et al. (2008, pp. 10–13).

[3] The typology reported in the table does not overlap neatly with the tripartite distinction between liberal, egalitarian and participatory conception of democracy that we follow in our empirical analysis (see Section 4). Nevertheless, these data show that factors related to social equality and institutional performance are more closely associated with the meaning of democracy than liberal values, especially in some countries.

This research has provided a first important overview of how Southeast Asians understand democracy, and it suggests that liberal values in this region may be more poorly consolidated than in others, such as Western or Latin American countries. It does, however, suffer from important shortcomings. First, the survey questions used to measure meanings of democracy require respondents to choose one or another option, instead of allowing that individuals may hold multiple conceptions of democracy or conflate them. First-priority questions such as those included in the Asian Barometer are useful to give an overview of what values are prioritized in democratic governance, but they may oversimplify the complexity of democratic attitudes. Studying public conceptions of democracy as complex cognitive structures is especially important in a region like Southeast Asia, where democratic and authoritarian notions of democracy coexist and blend in the minds of many citizens (Dore et al., 2014, pp. 42–5).

Second, it omits participation as a key dimension of democracy. To be sure, because of the above-mentioned prominent role of political elites in the region, scholars have often argued that informal participatory politics in Southeast Asia is feeble, and, to the extent that it takes place, it is often channelled through and constrained by state institutions (Jayasuriya & Rodan, 2007; Rodan, 2018). Yet, as we further discuss in the Section 2, many Southeast Asian countries do have a significant tradition of mass participation, especially during critical junctures that have helped to shape their political development. Omitting this dimension from the analysis therefore neglects an understanding of democracy that may resonate with many Southeast Asian citizens and have distinctive implications for political behaviour.

With a novel methodological approach and an in-depth analysis of democratic attitudes in Indonesia, Malaysia, the Philippines, Singapore and Thailand, this Element aims to refine and complete our understanding of popular conceptions of democracy in Southeast Asia by delivering *two main contributions*. First, we show that liberal understandings of democracy, while not predominant, are widespread and consequential in Southeast Asia. Especially in certain socio-demographic segments, liberal conceptions of democracy are common in the region, and they are closely intertwined with egalitarian/social conceptions. This is an important finding because, as we show later in this Element, liberal conceptions of democracy are significantly associated with support for democracy and political behaviour. Liberal democrats are more supportive of democracy as a political regime than any other group, but they are also more reluctant to participate in politics informally. This suggests that liberal democratic values, on the one hand, are crucial for democratic consolidation in Southeast Asia. On the other hand, however, liberal democrats will be less engaged in informal participation beyond elections, which is also an important dimension of democratic development.

Second, we bring participatory understandings of democracy into the analysis of democratic attitudes in the region. Here too, we show that this conception of democracy, while more poorly consolidated than liberal or egalitarian conceptions, has important implications for political behaviour. The most predictable finding is of course that participatory democrats tend to participate more in political activities beyond elections, which is consistent with our definition of participatory notions of democracy. But beyond that, and more interestingly, participatory democrats are also consistently more critical of the state of democracy and government institutions, even more so than liberal democrats. Studies of political culture in Southeast Asia often lament that the poor consolidation of liberal values is a key obstacle to democratic deepening in the region. Our findings, however, suggest that participatory understandings of democracy are more closely associated with critical evaluations of democracy. Democratic deepening in Southeast Asia would therefore benefit not only from further consolidation of liberal values, but also from a clearer understanding among mass publics that informal participation and public engagement are crucial to consolidate democratic accountability.

The remainder of this Element proceeds as follows. In the next section, we focus on the history of democratic development in Southeast Asia to provide qualitative context for our analysis. We then outline the conceptual and theoretical framework in Section 3, where we also describe our methodological approach and research design. Section 4 follows with empirical analysis of original survey data from the five Southeast Asian countries, and the final section concludes with a more exhaustive discussion of the findings and their implications.

2 Democracy in Southeast Asia

The research on popular conceptions of democracy in Southeast Asia reviewed in the previous section provides a first overview of how ordinary people understand democracy in this region. As we mentioned, the prevailing view that emerges from this scholarship is that liberal ideas of democracy, in which democracy is understood as protection of individual freedoms and checks and balances to constrain the executive, are not firmly rooted in Southeast Asian political culture. Many citizens, when asked to make a choice, tend to identify democracy in terms of its social–egalitarian component. At the same time, however, this overview is incomplete, as it overlooks important dimensions of democracy and oversimplifies the structure of democratic attitudes.

In this section, we aim to provide a more comprehensive contextualization of Southeast Asia in the debate on democratic development and democratic attitudes. To do so, we start with a brief study of aggregate-level patterns of democratic development in the region, as captured by quantitative indicators. We leverage the widely used Varieties of Democracy (V-Dem) indexes of electoral, liberal, egalitarian and participatory democracy to show how these various dimensions of democracy evolve over time. We identify some common patterns in the region and how they differ from those observed in the rest of the world, and we discuss differences among the five selected countries in how democratic institutions have evolved over time. We then complement the quantitative data with historical, qualitative profiles of the trajectory of democracy development in each country. This allows us to add substance and in-depth understanding to the macro-level patterns identified by democratic indexes, as we focus especially on how ideas of democracy have been defined and propagated by political elites, as well as on patterns of contentions surrounding democratic ideals.

Before we proceed, a brief note is in order about case selection. Southeast Asia is a highly diverse region comprising eleven countries with highly different levels of democracy, from Brunei's closed autocracy to the vibrant, if imperfect, democracy of Indonesia. Many of its countries, as we further discuss in Section 2.1, are not clear-cut cases of either democracy or autocracy, and could best be characterized as hybrid regimes that blend elements of authoritarianism and democracy. Furthermore, democratic development in the region may display substantial variation in regime features over time, in what could be described as democratic 'careening' (Slater, 2013), and a process of democratic backsliding has developed over the past few years (Haggard & Kaufman, 2021; Pepinsky, 2017). This institutional make-up sets the region apart from the cases most frequently studied in the literature, where democracy is typically considered 'the only game in town'. It suggests that Southeast Asia may be an especially fruitful ground to study how different – and possibly conflicting – ideas of democracy may be available and consequential in the minds of citizens, either as coherent constructs or as more fluid and complex sets of attitudes.

2.1 Macro-Level Patterns

Figure 1 allows us to put our five cases in a global comparative perspective, as it analyses the evolution of the four democracy dimensions identified: electoral, liberal, egalitarian and participatory, with data from the V-Dem project (Lindberg et al., 2014).[4] In panel (a), the curves track the average of each dimension for all the world countries included in the data set, excluding the five under analysis (Indonesia, Malaysia, the Philippines, Singapore and Thailand). Panel (b)

---

[4] These data are based on a survey of international experts who are asked to evaluate the various dimensions of democracy in their countries or region of expertise.

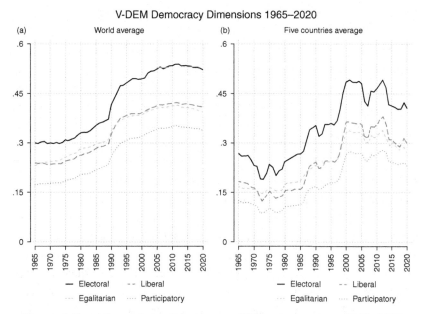

Figure 1 Four dimensions of democracy (V-Dem) over time, 1965–2020

presents instead the evolution of the mean values for the five countries under study. Each dimension average ranges from 0 to 1, where lower values denote worse levels of democratic performance, as seen by the experts interviewed by this international data collection programme.

There are a few elements worth highlighting in this comparison. The first is that, in our five countries, as in the world average panel, average values for all dimensions appear to be rather similar, and are modest overall. For example, on a scale ranging from 0 to 1, the electoral dimension index for 2020 scores an average value of 0.51 in panel (a), and is only slightly lower in the five Southeast Asian cases, above 0.40. This reassures us that the five cases we have selected – although somewhat underperforming in their democratic electoral dimension when compared with the rest of the world – can nevertheless be considered quite 'typical' in their democratic performance. To be sure, many observations in the sample have extreme values. Democracies such as Sweden or Denmark, for instance, consistently score above 0.9, while autocracies such as China or Qatar rarely reach even 0.1 on the very same scale. But on average, the world – just like the Southeast Asian countries that we study – does not tend to resemble such clear-cut cases, as it appears to fluctuate around grey or hybrid areas.[5]

---

[5] For example, of the 179 countries for which V-DEM provided a value on the electoral dimension, 53 countries range between 0 and 0.33, while 56 states are above 0.66. The remaining 70 countries – including Mexico, Poland, Colombia, Maldives, Bhutan and Hungary – range

Analysing the attitudes towards dimensions of democracy in Southeast Asia is thus not only useful for the five countries we directly observe, but it may also offer valuable insights for other cases with a similar institutional outlook.

Second, in both panels, a substantial difference can be observed between the electoral dimension and the other three: the electoral democracy line is consistently higher, regardless of the specific historical period considered. As the theoretical and empirical literature on democracy would suggest, electoral democracy is relatively easy to achieve, whereas other important dimensions remain elusive. Democratic performance appears especially modest when evaluated through the lens of a participatory understanding of democracy, as scores for this dimension trail all others, while the liberal and egalitarian evolve almost simultaneously. And again, when we compare the two panels in this respect, the five countries we have selected for study look remarkably similar to the rest of the world. In our five Southeast Asian cases too, electoral democracy has often been within reach over the past twenty years; however, the scoreboard is more disappointing when we assess these countries by their ability to develop a 'fuller', stable democracy that encompasses liberal, social and participatory elements.

Finally, some observations concern the trajectory over time of aggregate-level democracy scores, taking 1965, the first year in which all the five cases were independent countries, as the starting point. In the 1970s, democracy has made substantial progress in many countries, as illustrated in Figure 1(a). The average values of our five countries suggest a similar pattern, although it is worth noting that the increase in values from the mid-1980s to the late 1990s is driven by democratic transitions in the Philippines and Indonesia. We should also note, however, the substantial decline in aggregate scores in recent years, which is consistent with the so-called wave of autocratization that has been identified in the comparative literature (Lührmann & Lindberg, 2019). These longitudinal trends indicate how the various dimensions of democracy can change substantially over time in response to changes in the political landscape (which we further describe in Section 2.2) and again reflect a close relationship between the patterns observed in our five cases and those observed elsewhere in the world. The extent of democratic backsliding, however, does appear to be more pronounced in our five countries than in the rest of the world. After a peak of 0.49 in 2012, for example, the electoral democracy score has dropped

---

between those values. Relatedly, if, rather than relying on V-DEM, we rely on other indexes such as Polity or Freedom House, the results are similar, which indicates the reliability of the data. We do not use Polity IV or FH because the former provides only an overall score on its index, ranging from −10 to +10, while the latter is composed of two indicators that touch upon dimensions of freedom: political rights and civil liberties.

dramatically to 0.40, and so have all other indexes, at least in part due to the establishment of military rule in Thailand the following year. In short, Figure 1 shows contiguity between the five Southeast Asian cases and global patterns, but it also suggests that understanding the dynamics of specific countries within this small pool is crucial to get a sense of Southeast Asia as a whole.

To this end, we now turn to analysing the evolution of the electoral, liberal, egalitarian and participatory democratic dimensions for the five countries individually since gaining independence,[6] as shown in the five charts included in Figure 2. As in Figure 1, there are two patterns that are consistent across the panels. First, the electoral dimension is consistently the highest performing in all five cases. Second, as pointed out earlier, all four dimensions behave in synchrony, showing that they are correlated; that is, improvements or deteriorations in one dimension are reflected in all dimensions.[7] Third, every country shows its own ranking of the various dimensions. The electoral dimension is the highest performing in every country; however, the participatory performs worst in Singapore, but does much better in Indonesia, Malaysia and the Philippines. By contrast, the egalitarian dimension is the lowest-performing in the Philippines, whereas it ranks second in Malaysia and Singapore. This suggests that disaggregating democratic performance in its various dimensions can reveal interesting differences across these five cases.

As for the development over time of the various democratic dimensions, Figure 2 shows striking differences among the five cases which highlight the different political evolution of each country. Singapore appears to be a case of exceptional authoritarian stability, as all of its scores have changed little in the past fifty years. Malaysia, for its part, appears to be a fairly stable case in democratic development, especially the last third of the period, with a spike towards a more democratic political system occurring at the end of the time series following the 2018 elections. Indonesia has been the best-performing case on all dimensions following its transition from authoritarianism in the late 1990s. The Philippines has similarly witnessed a large increase in its democratic scores following a democratic transition in the second half of the 1980s, although its scores have declined markedly in the last five years. Finally, Thailand follows an irregular trajectory marked by dramatic upward and downward swings, which have resulted from repeated interruptions of democratic rule by the military. Beyond these broad strokes emerging from quantitative democracy scores, qualitative nuance is needed to gain a better understanding of

---

[6] Except for Thailand that was never colonized. We take 1945 as the departure point.

[7] Given that V-Dem indexes are based on expert opinions, however, one should bear in mind the possibility that such high levels of correlations may reflect expert beliefs that all dimensions of democracy are inextricably linked.

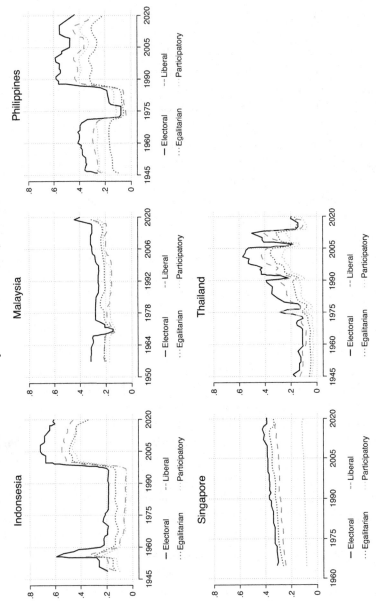

Figure 2 Democratic development in five Southeast Asian countries (V-Dem dimensions)

each country's democratic development and discourse on democracy. The historical profiles in the next section aim to provide such insight.

2.2 Historical Trajectories

The patterns of political development identified in Section 2.1 paint an overall picture of Southeast Asia as a region in which democratic institutions are poorly consolidated. At the same time, however, this generalization overlooks the substantial variation over time and across cases in democratic practice displayed in Figure 2. Democratic development in the region has therefore been shaped by both a common, general weakness of democratic norms and practices and country-specific historical vicissitudes. We now delve into the historical trajectories of political development in our five case studies. Although the factors we emphasize vary somewhat from one country to another, we focus especially on how democratic and authoritarian forces have interacted to define those countries' political dynamics and the discourse about democracy, which in turn is closely intertwined with institutional formation. These historical insights shed light on the key processes that have produced the macro-level patterns captured by the expert scores discussed in the previous section, and they also provide the necessary qualitative context for the quantitative analysis performed later in this Element.

2.2.1 Indonesia

Indonesia is often described as the world's third-largest democracy, and indeed it has the highest democracy scores out of the five countries we have selected. However, few scholars of Indonesia would characterize this country as a 'full' or 'liberal' democracy, as democratic practices in this country present substantial flaws. Despite Indonesia's official status as a (relatively) young democracy, democracy in fact has a long history in this country. The first universal democratic elections took place in 1955 (or about five years after the end of the Indonesian National Revolution), yet interest in the Western concept of democracy among Indonesian intellectual elites was already well established by the time a nationalist movement started to emerge in the early twentieth century. The implementation in the early 1900s of the Ethical Policy, which was intended to promote a more equitable and inclusive model colonial rule, was an especially important development. Although this initiative may have failed to substantially ameliorate the material conditions of the Indonesian population, its educational component successfully fostered awareness of the injustice of the colonial project and familiarized younger Indonesians with ideas of freedom, democracy and self-determination (Vickers, 2013).

Against this background, the nationalist movement that challenged Dutch colonization in the 1920s and 1930s had a distinctively democratic, inclusionary and participatory character – although not necessarily a liberal one. On the one hand, a substantial component of the nationalist movement was Islamist in ideology (Laffan, 2003). As much as these leaders may have envisioned the new nation as a democratic community, they also believed that such a community should be established on Islamic principles. Therefore, this strand of thoughts rejected certain key liberal principles – most notably, that state and religion should be separate and that no religion should hold a privileged position above any other. On the other hand, the more pluralistically inclined political elites, who eventually dominated the nationalist movement and politics in the newly independent Indonesia, were not especially committed to liberal tenets either. Few among them believed in a Western-style political system with a prominent role for the legislative branch and the checks and balances typical of a liberal democracy (Feith, 1962). After the 1955 elections, the high level of political polarization and mobilization – as well as an increasingly influential role for the army – ushered in the collapse of Indonesia's fledgling democracy. Sukarno himself eventually dismantled this 'liberal' political system, leading Indonesia into the tumultuous authoritarian years of so-called Guided Democracy.

The tragic transition to Indonesia's 'New Order' brought about a renewed emphasis on *Pancasila*, Indonesia's 'national ideology', as the moral foundation of the Indonesian state. This loose ideology includes five principles: belief in one God, justice and civility among people, unity of Indonesia, democracy through deliberation and consensus among representatives, and social justice for the people. It is telling that none of these five principles, which were established in 1945, emphasizes liberal ideas such as individual rights and freedoms, or the importance of popular participation. Instead, the idea of democracy that transpires from these five tenets is closer to what some have described as 'organicist' political thought (Bourchier, 2014), which rejects adversarial, Western-style political competition and accountability in favour of a more hierarchical, paternalistic relationship between citizens and their representatives. *Pancasila* therefore stresses ideas of democracy rooted in the deliberative, consensual and social tradition, and excludes more explicitly liberal and participatory elements.

Following Suharto's resignation in 1998, Indonesia entered a period of reform that introduced genuinely liberal features in Indonesia's political system. Under the leadership of B.J. Habibie, Indonesia again became a democracy – one that featured free and fair elections, a system of free media, provisions for civil and political rights, and new state architecture that emphasized regional autonomy. After three decades of stifling authoritarian rule, Indonesians also finally enjoyed new opportunities for political participation: the old divide between pluralism and Islamism again took the centre of the political stage (King, 2003); civil society organizations and student-led groups, which had been an important factor in authoritarian decline and breakdown (Aspinall, 2005), became more assertive; electoral participation was exceptionally high with a turnout above 90%; and a former opposition figure (and daughter of Sukarno – Megawati) led her party to an electoral victory. This movement, called *Reformasi*, therefore coincided with a re-emergence of the democratic, inclusive and participatory traditions of Indonesian political history.

Today, the hopeful, bold years of *Reformasi* are only a distant memory for many Indonesians, and democracy in this country seems to have lost momentum for further consolidation and deepening. To be sure, as mentioned above, Indonesia still has a more-than-respectable democratic record, especially when appraised from a comparative perspective. Nevertheless, after several years marked by a normalization of politics, widespread clientelism and stagnation of civil rights, Indonesia's democracy has begun to regress in the eyes of many observers (Mietzner, 2018; Power & Warburton, 2020). In terms of conceptions of democracy, one of the most interesting trends in recent years seems to be the resurgence of more illiberal, nativist ideas of democracy, as political Islam seems to have gained renewed political influence (Fossati, forthcoming). This development, together with other worrying trends such as executive overreach, has once again emphasized the frailty of liberal political culture in this country. At the same time, however, it should be emphasized that Indonesians are divided on the issue of state–Islam relations, as many of its citizens, although they are a minority, do hold pluralist views (Fossati, 2019). Therefore, there is in Indonesia – as in most societies – evidence of a significant degree of heterogeneity in terms of liberal values, understandings of democracy and evaluation of democratic institutions.

2.2.2 Malaysia

Since gaining its independence from British rule in the late 1950s, Malaysia has had a remarkably stable political regime, as shown in Figure 2. Perhaps the most distinctive feature of the Malaysian political system, when compared with the other four cases that we study in this Element, is its salience of ethnicity, which has informed ideas and practices of democracy in a diverse society where Muslim Malays constitute the dominant group. Throughout Malaysia's history, its politics have been characterized by a tension between the aspiration to include various ethnic groups in the political process, on the one hand – and, on the other, a reality in which Malay supremacy has been sanctioned with various forms of 'special rights' that grant Malays racial privileges over the two other major groups, namely Chinese and Indian Malaysians.

Because of the centrality of ethnicity, as well as a legacy of ethic animosity and conflict, early Malaysian ideas of democracy had a strong emphasis on consociationalism (Lijphart, 1969). The initial push for a consociational view of democracy could be attributed to the first prime minister of Malaysia, Tunku Abdul Rahman, who managed to form a pan-ethnic political coalition that would provide a basic model for the future decades. The basic idea of consociational democracy is that majority rule alone is insufficient to provide stability and peace in societies marked by deep ethnic cleavages. To mitigate the risk that ethnic tensions may escalate into conflict, political elites engage in cooperative agreements in which all major ethnic groups are represented, so that each group has access to a fair share of the resources that come with political power, and the points of view of all ethnic groups are heard when political decisions are made. To be sure, the political landscape changed significantly after the 1960s, when Malays established a more clearly dominant position over other ethnic groups (Musolf & Springer, 1979). Yet this Malay-dominated view of consociationalism has remained a deep-rooted and much-debated idea of democracy in this country (Mauzy, 2013), and the *Barisan Nasional* (BN), the grand coalition that dominated Malaysian politics until 2018 was constituted by parties representing the three main ethnic groups, led by the United Malays National Organization (UMNO).

This conception of democracy – with its emphasis on groups rather than individuals, and on an ascriptive trait such as ethnicity rather than universal rights and equality before the law – is a substantial departure from liberal democratic ideals. In the context of Malaysian politics, this point has not been lost to ruling political elites, who have used various incarnations of consociationalism to justify the authoritarianism of the Malaysian political regime. Supporters of the BN system argued that consociationalism – coupled with a rejection of a liberal, Western-style model of democracy based on civil liberties and individual rights – was necessary to maintain racial harmony and stability, as well as economic development, in such a diverse society. The enduring stability of this conceptualization and discourse about democracy went hand-in-hand with a stable, authoritarian political system in which these ideas were propagated through a tightly controlled media system and electoral competition was suppressed with gerrymandering and other expedients (Case, 2013).

The 2018 elections, in which the BN suffered a surprise defeat, presented an unprecedented opportunity to reform Malaysian politics in a more liberal direction (Nadzri, 2018). Indeed, the newly elected leaders, sustained by ebullient mass mobilization and civil society activism (Weiss, 2021), put forward plans to introduce policies and practices that have long been a hallmark of parliamentary and liberal democracy, such as freedom of press, free and unbiased elections, or a more egalitarian distribution of responsibilities in the executive and judicial sphere. However, in less than two years, the new coalition collapsed due to internal power struggles, paving the way for a return to power for many influential BN figures and a more majoritarian vision of democracy among Malay parties.

These recent developments vividly illustrate the complexity and the challenges of supporting a democratic, liberal agenda in a context where liberal ideas and practices are not widespread, and where the formation of heterogeneous coalitions is necessary to govern (Dettman, 2020). Yet, the 2018 elections are also a reminder that in Malaysia, there exists a substantial level of demand for a more liberal, democratic regime, despite the paralysing legacy of sixty years of authoritarianism and a pervasive public discourse in which 'Western' liberal values are routinely marginalized and belittled. Despite the constraints imposed by still authoritarian formal institutions (Giersdorf & Croissant, 2011), informal participation – for example, through civil society organization or in the form of the mass protests during the Asian Financial Crisis and in the already mentioned run-up to the 2018 elections – has played a key role in advocating for this agenda (Hassan & Weiss, 2012; Weiss, 2006).

2.2.3 The Philippines

The Philippines is the first Southeast Asian country to have achieved independence from colonial rule, as the United States recognized the independence of their former colony shortly after the end of World War II. Although centuries of Spanish domination left a deep mark on Filipino society and culture, the democratic institutions installed upon independence in 1946 were inspired by the American tradition of liberal democracy. The constitution provided for a democratic, presidential republic with a bicameral system and three separate, independent branches of government. On paper, then, liberal ideas of democracy were crucial in shaping the architecture of democracy in the Philippines. However, as it is often the case when institutions are installed in new contexts with significant adaptations to local specificities (Diamond, 1992), democratic practice in the Philippines has often departed from the liberal canon.

A striking feature of economic and social life in the Philippines is its very high level of inequality, which has been a powerful force in shaping this country's politics. Writing in the aftermath of the collapse of Ferdinand Marcos' dictatorship, Benedict Anderson (1988) famously described the Philippines as a '*cacique* democracy' to emphasize the stark asymmetries between voters and their representatives. Centuries of colonial rule, both Spanish and American, had nurtured an influential class of local economic elites who swiftly captured political power at the moment of decolonization and managed to further entrench their rule in the following decades. These elites have positioned themselves as the *de facto* oligarchy of Filipino politics and society – and democracy in the Philippines, although liberal in name, has consequently suffered from low levels of participation and competitiveness. Whereas politics in other countries have often featured important debates on religious or ideological cleavages, Filipino political elites have been typically indistinguishable in their outlook on social and political issues, and linkages between citizens and politicians have been highly clientelistic (Teehankee, 2012). Elections, especially in some regions, have often been marred by vote-buying, intimidation and violence.

With such a discrepancy between the promise of liberal democratic institutions and the political practices that they allow, it is no surprise that many Filipino citizens may not feel a strong attachment to a liberal conception of democracy. Most political elites, for their part, despite being staunchly democratic and liberal in name, are often sceptical of popular participation, frequently disparaging ordinary Filipinos as being unable to understand the concept of democracy and tending to offer their votes to the highest bidder (May & Selochan, 2004, p. 63). The ordinary people themselves, who have been regularly disappointed by the unfulfilled promises of liberal democracy, have at times been supportive of developments that challenge political elites and their liberal ideology, such as increased involvement of the military in politics, extra-judicial violence, scathing populist rhetoric and authoritarian turns. Rodrigo Duterte's meteoric rise to prominence in national politics over the last decade is only the most recent example of this tension between liberal ideas of democracy – endorsed by social and cultural elites – and a more 'social' understanding of democracy that resonates more closely with most Filipino citizens. Duterte's bloody war on drugs, for instance, might have been utterly abhorrent from a liberal perspective (Thompson, 2016), but the very high levels of public support that it enjoyed indicate that most Filipinos evaluated this policy favourably in terms of its possible social outcomes.

The case of the Philippines therefore presents a paradox of sorts: liberal democratic institutions were established early on and fully (at least in form), but they have functioned in such a flawed manner that, ironically, they may have contributed to the weakness of liberal values observed in the region. Perhaps more than in other Southeast Asian countries, in the Philippines there appears to be an interplay between conceptions of democracy and social class, as the liberal ideas of democracy have long been used by elites to legitimize a political system that has delivered few tangible benefits to Filipinos of more modest social conditions.

Finally, it should be noted that, like Indonesia and Malaysia, the Philippines do have an important history of participatory politics. As mentioned, political institutions in this country offer few opportunities for participation through formal channels, which tend to be tightly controlled by elites. Yet there have been notable episodes of informal mass mobilization in politics at crucial moments, such as in the uprisings that coincided with the end of the Marcos regime in 1986 or the protests against President Estrada in 2001. Furthermore, civil society organizations have long been present and active in a wide range of policy areas (Clarke, 2006). It is therefore plausible that public participation – and informal participation especially – may be considered by some Filipinos to be vital for democracy.

2.2.4 Singapore

A key juncture in Singapore's history as an independent country was its 1965 expulsion from Malaysia. It left Singapore – a small, ethnically divided country – to fend for itself with few natural or human resources. This traumatic separation was due in no small part to divergent views between Malaysian and Singaporean leaders about ethnic relations, a theme that is closely intertwined with ideas of democracy. Although Malaysia supported the consociational model described above, in which Malays maintained special privileges, the Singaporean elite, mostly British-educated, insisted on the liberal principle that every citizen should be equal before the law, regardless of their ethnic background (Barr, 2019). This principle was especially important for Singapore, a Chinese-majority society whose ethnic make-up differed sharply from the rest of Malaysia. Eventually, the tension between the two goals – enjoying the security and economic advantages of the Malaysian federation and maintaining a system in which no ethnicity would be privileged – proved to be irreconcilable.

Although this background suggests a certain ideological commitment to at least some liberal ideals, it was also clear by the mid-1960s that the emerging Singaporean political class did not see Western-style democracy as a political model for their community. During the years following the 1959 elections, the newly established Singaporean government, under the leadership of Lee Kuan Yew and his People's Action Party (PAP), moved swiftly to suppress political competition by crippling the ability of the leftist opposition to mobilize through labour unions and intimidating or arresting its leaders (Thum, 2013). Such initiatives were justified as necessary to maintain internal security against a communist threat, and the idea that authoritarianism was needed to preserve social order in the new and possibly unstable nation was even more forcefully reiterated after the expulsion from Malaysia in 1965, which created a new situation of vulnerability that Lee and others exploited to consolidate their rule.

These early developments were foundational in establishing a political model that still characterizes contemporary Singapore. Although Singaporeans enjoy some individual liberal rights in the civil and economic spheres, political participation and competition show the patterns of authoritarian politics. The PAP, which has ruled the country since the establishment of the Republic of Singapore in 1965, maintains complete control of the executive and the state apparatus, including the ostensibly independent legislative and judicial branches (Mutalib, 2000); all media are controlled by the government, and elections, although free of fraud, are widely seen as unfair. Political development in Singapore has therefore blended liberal and authoritarian elements in a political regime that has remained stable from its inception in the early 1960s to today.

Another distinctive feature of Singaporean narratives about democracy is the strong emphasis on communitarianism, especially starting from the 1980s (Chua, 1997). As the urgency of the security threats of the Cold War started to wane and Singapore's economic success gave rise to a well-educated, consumeristic middle class, Singaporean leaders started to worry that the legitimacy of their rule might be weakened and that the newly found economic prosperity might bring about a cultural shift towards Western ideas of individualism and liberalism. The counter-narrative developed to avert these outcomes pitted Asian and Western societies against each other, and contended that the former were more conservative, traditional, and appreciative of social harmony, a goal to which individual rights and political contentiousness should be subordinated. Lee was one of the most articulate proponents of the idea that democracy should not be understood as a 'one-size-fits-all' concept, and that Asian societies present a cultural preference for communitarianism that makes the individual-based Western–liberal democracy unsuitable for these contexts (Zakaria & Yew, 1994). This 'Asian values' narrative, popularized in the 1990s by authoritarian leaders in Asia, thus stems from a politically motivated desire to find a reason to legitimize the authoritarian nature of their government, while concomitantly presenting an oversimplified image of a homogenous and harmonious society (Means, 1996). This ideological legacy may have weakened liberal understandings of democracy among Singaporean citizens.

A final note should be added about the participatory dimension of democracy. As the charts in Figure 2 show, Singapore's record in the participatory sphere is dismal; its score ranks lowest among the five countries and is on par with that of Thailand, a country classified in 2020 as a military authoritarian regime. Although various civil society groups have long been active in Singapore and have sought to influence policy-making (Ortmann, 2015), most observers understand public participation as a marginal element in this country's politics, or emphasize the regime's ability to harness tightly controlled modes of participation to further consolidate authoritarian politics (Rodan, 2018). Political elites have at times tried to justify their suppression of participation avenues by blaming the citizens themselves, citing unsubstantiated claims that the public is uninformed and unenlightened and that citizens are happy to give up certain personal freedoms in favour of socio-economic stability (Ho, 2003). Such elitist stereotypes resonate with those observed in other Southeast Asian cases, but it is especially interesting that in Singapore they have persisted despite high levels of socioeconomic development and educational attainment among the local population (Lai, 2019).

2.2.5 Thailand

As shown in Figure 2, democratic development in Thailand has followed a path marked by a series of discontinuities and setbacks since the 1970s. To understand the historical background that has framed these dynamics, we must appreciate the role of the military and the monarchy, two key players in modern Thai politics. The monarchy, especially starting from the reformist rule of Chulalongkorn (1868–1910), has had a central role in transforming Thailand from a feudal to a modern society and a nation-state. This support for economic and social modernization, however, was not coupled with advocacy for a democratic system of government featuring liberal checks and balances. Although Thailand today is a constitutional monarchy in name, the sustained involvement of the royal palace in ordinary politics, both during democratic periods and under the various military-led regimes that have characterized Thai political history, has made it clear that the authority of the monarchy exists independently from what the constitution provides (Ferrara, 2015, p. 2).

To consolidate their rule and an illiberal notion of democracy, Thai monarchs have relied on appeals based on national and religious (Buddhist) identity, which have contributed to propagating understandings of democracy that sharply build on ideas based on liberalism. Buddhist cosmology, in particular, which presents a hierarchical view of the cosmological order, has justified political inequalities and presented them as natural and desirable (Connors, 2007, p. 105). The idea of a cosmologically derived political order has been closely associated with discourse about so-called 'Thai-style democracy', an authoritarian, paternalistic political system with the king as the head of state in which virtuous and religious elites rule for the good of the people while being sheltered from electoral accountability.

Powerful royalist actors, with the support of the military, have therefore had an important role in shaping public discourse on democracy (Ferrara, 2015). These powerful forces have long sought to promote an image of the king as a custodian of democracy, an impartial and morally superior guardian who may not be involved in the ugliness of day-to-day politics, but would intervene to protect democratic institutions in exceptional circumstances (Tejapira, 2016). In fact, monarchical power in contemporary Thailand has authoritarian origins. The monarchy, after a decline in royal power following a bloodless coup in 1932 that imposed constitutional constraints on royal prerogatives, started to rise again as a powerful political actor in the 1950s – and especially under the rule of Sarit Thanarat, the general who seized power in 1957, suspended the constitution and initiated a period of highly repressive and authoritarian military rule. Monarchy revival was instrumental to this reactionary political project, and throughout the ensuing decades, the royal palace would often manifest a preference for maintaining law and order rather than consolidating democratic institutions (Hewison, 1997). In recent years, royalists have further demonstrated their authoritarian tendency by relying on a conservative judiciary to overturn democratic elections (McCargo, 2020) and by consolidating their anti-democratic alliance with the military (Chambers & Waitoolkiat, 2016).

This mainstream, authoritarian view of democracy propagated by the monarchy, however, has been controversial throughout Thai history, as Thai citizens have been divided about the role of the monarchy and the powers it should have. On the one hand, Thai politics, during democratic periods, has featured high levels of political polarization since the mid-2000s, when Prime Minister Thaksin Shinawatra rose to power in what was seen as a challenge to royalist power (Sinpeng, 2021). In contrast to the royalist establishment, supporters of Thaksin and his party, although not necessarily liberal, have consistently supported an electoral view of democracy and advocated the return to free and fair elections (Norton, 2012). It should also be noted that the political platform developed by this group has included important social elements as well. Thaksin supporters were concentrated in the lower social classes and the poorest regions of the north and the northeast of the country (Hewison, 2012), which had not benefitted as much as other regions from Thailand's decades of sustained economic development. The idea of democracy articulated by this group could thus be described as a blend of electoral and egalitarian elements.

On the other hand, more liberal and participatory notions of democracy have recently become more salient in Thailand, especially as student-led pro-democracy protests have explicitly called for a reform of the monarchy (Sombatpoonsiri, 2021). Initially triggered by the dissolution in February 2020 of the Future Forward Party, which had been critical of military rule, protesters went on to identify monarchy reform as one of their demands in August of that year. They submitted to the government a list of demands for reform, which included items such as revoking the king's immunity against lawsuits, constraining the king's ability to comment on political issues and allowing a comprehensive audit of royal assets. Support for this agenda may be limited to a narrow socio-demographic segment, but these developments are further evidence of the existence of a liberal streak in Thai understandings of democracy. As in the past, when political competition was constrained by authoritarian institutions, some Thais, especially from younger generations, have found meaning in informal participation channels.

3 Conceptualizing and Measuring the Meaning of Democracy

Political scientists often distinguish between various types of democratic regimes to account for the vast diversity in political institutions and practices found among the many countries that could be considered democratic. Although various typologies have been proposed, an especially influential dichotomy distinguishes between *electoral* and *liberal* democracies (Diamond, 1999, 2002). At a minimum, as suggested by proponents of a 'minimalist' definition of democracy (Przeworski et al., 2000), a democracy must be an electoral democracy, with free and fair elections and adequate levels of political compe-tition. Yet modern democracies are also supposed to be liberal – referring to political regimes that limit the power of electoral majorities with various types of checks and balances to protect individual and minority rights (Fawcett, 2018). Against this background, many have studied, both conceptually and empirically, the various forms that democracy can assume when reasonably competitive elections occur but liberal values are poorly consolidated (Collier & Levitsky, 1997; Hamid, 2014; O'Donnell, 1994; Zakaria, 2007).

This focus on liberal values in academic research, however, does not imply that citizens primarily understand democracy in liberal terms. As many scholars have pointed out, ordinary citizens may hold different conceptions of what it means to be a democracy (Huber et al., 1997; Lindberg et al., 2014). Besides the obvious requirement of free and fair elections, and the more elusive and contentious emphasis on liberal constitutional arrangements and protections for minorities, democracy can be understood, for example, in *deliberative* terms. From this perspective, government should be guided by reason, and its decisions should be reached through a process of dialogue and compromise rather than by appealing to emotions and identities (Cohen, 1997; Fishkin, 1991). Others have articulated a *participatory* notion of democracy, stressing the importance of citizen involvement in democratic politics beyond the formal channels provided by delegation to elected representatives (Barber, 2003). For those relying on a *majoritarian* principle, democracy is condensed into the idea that the will of the majority should be sovereign, and that democracy is ensured when the will of the many prevails over the will of the few. In contrast, the *consensual* principle advocates building a broad base of support for public policy, and it encourages institutions to be inclusive of as many political perspectives as possible (Lijphart, 1969). Finally, an *egalitarian* or *social* conception of democracy acknowledges the importance of material and immaterial inequalities and asks whether all citizens are equally empowered to participate in, and benefit from, democratic politics (Huber et al., 1997; Young, 2002).[8]

Such a multidimensional conceptualization of democracy has important implications for democratic legitimacy and for the current debate on democratic backsliding. Because individuals may harbour different views and expectations of what democracy is, they may hold democratic practice to different standards and formulate diverging evaluations of whether democracy is 'delivering' (Canache et al., 2001; Norris, 2011). Understanding conceptions of democracy is therefore essential to identifying public expectations and pockets of discontent with democratic performance that may lead to questioning the legitimacy of democratic institutions.

The remainder of this section offers a review of existing research and outlines the conceptual framework that will guide the empirical analysis presented in the next section. We start with some general remarks about the role of ordinary people in democracy, as well as a more specific discussion of the relationship between democratic attitudes and political regimes. Following this, we conceptualize democracy as a complex, multidimensional construct. Drawing from existing research, we focus especially on liberal, participatory and social–egalitarian understandings of democracy as the main dimensions of democracy that we will examine in this Element. We then review the studies that have analysed the implications of such multidimensional conceptualization of

---

[8] The above-mentioned principles do not limit all the democracy conceptions. They are some of the most relevant, but not the only ones.

democracy, particularly for democratic satisfaction and the legitimacy of democratic institutions. Finally, we outline our methodological approach and research design.

3.1 Ordinary People and Democracy

In studying popular conceptions of democracy, this Element emphasizes the importance of understanding public opinion, especially with reference to how democracy is conceptualized and evaluated by ordinary people. This is a different approach from the one followed by most contemporary literature on democracy, which has focused especially on the study of political institutions and elites. Yet in prioritizing the study of democratic attitudes among mass publics, we build on various scholarly works that have posited and demonstrated, from various perspectives, that ordinary people play an important role in preserving democratic institutions.

The first strand of this literature can be traced back to the idea that democratization results from structural factors, specifically from modernization processes that are closely linked to a cultural transformation in mass publics (Inglehart, 1997). The socioeconomic changes brought about by modernization (especially urbanization and rising levels of education) favour the rise of a more informed citizenry who are better able to articulate democratic political demands and to fight for them, which eventually facilitates democratization (Welzel & Inglehart, 2008). In terms of cultural change, the increasing availability of material resources – which is a typical feature of industrial and post-industrial societies – is coupled with the emergence of self-expression values that are foundational to liberal democracy. Although this approach has fallen somewhat out of favour in our era of democratic backsliding, its proponents insist that it remains a valid approach to studying democracy and its changes over time (Welzel, 2021). Along the same lines, recent research has suggested that democratic institutions are more resilient when citizens are supportive of democracy (Claassen, 2020). This resonates with the idea that democracy, to be fully consolidated, needs to be perceived not only as a viable and desirable regime form, but as 'the only game in town' (Linz & Stepan, 1996).

A second strand of research departs from the assumption that democratic values are key for democratic development, but focuses more closely on explaining variation in such democratic attitudes. Satisfaction with democracy can vary substantially across time and place, and this variation cannot be explained solely based on broad patterns of modernization and secularization. Since the seminal work by Easton (1975) many researchers have explored the insight that public support for any political regime depends on its performance or its ability to deliver outcomes that are valued by its citizens (Norris, 2011). When a democracy delivers public goods such as security, economic growth and a range of social, civil and political rights, citizens are more likely to appreciate the value of democracy and prefer it to authoritarian alternatives. By contrast, when democracies fail to deliver, public dissatisfaction in democratic institutions and practices may grow, and such disillusionment may even extend to democratic principles (Rohrschneider, 2002). Empirical research has indeed found that support for democracy is influenced by government performance in both developed and young democracies alike (Magalhães, 2014; Mattes & Bratton, 2007). Other scholars have focused on satisfaction with democracy and observed that it is affected by factors such as economic performance (Cordero & Simón, 2016; Kriesi, 2018), procedural fairness (Magalhães, 2016), provision of public safety (Fernandez & Kuenzi, 2010), the effectiveness of bureaucrats and officials (Ariely, 2013) and the delivery of 'political' goods such as freedom and accountability (Huang et al., 2008).

This research has studied the complex interplay between how democratic institutions perform, how citizens evaluate them and the prospects for democratic durability itself. The patterns uncovered in these studies suggest that citizens may play a crucial role not only in democratization and democratic transitions, but also in more 'normal' periods of democratic politics – as lack of public support for, or satisfaction with, democracy may have detrimental effects for democratic governance. In well-established democracies, for instance, widespread dissatisfaction with democracy may pave the way for the emergence of authoritarian or populist actors; in young democracies, poorly established democratic values may hinder significant progress towards the transition to a liberal democratic regime. In other words, democracies, like any regime, are more stable when they enjoy high levels of legitimacy, or when they benefit from the belief that existing political institutions are the most appropriate or proper ones for the society (Lipset, 1959). Moreover, when a democracy performs well, its citizens are more likely to perceive it as a legitimate regime.

In short, democracies need committed democrats in order to survive and thrive. Democratic regimes typically stipulate a series of constitutional provisions as well as checks and balances to avoid regressing into authoritarianism. Yet, ultimately, the observance of the form and substance of such rules rests on the informal social norms that underpin them (Helmke & Levitsky, 2006). Politicians may challenge these norms in an attempt to aggrandize their own power, especially in the subtle, gradual fashion that is typical of contemporary patterns of democratic backsliding (Bermeo, 2016; Curato & Fossati, 2020). Citizens need to be aware of these attempts and must be willing to punish (most notably, with their vote) potentially authoritarian political elites for their anti-democratic behaviour. This is not always an easy task for voters. For example, recent experimental research has shown that, in both old and new democracies, partisan polarization may compromise voters' willingness to rebuke attacks on democratic principles (Fossati et al., 2022; Graham & Svolik, 2020). In any case, democratic values are foundational informal norms for democratic institutions, and their implementation requires a concerted effort by elites and ordinary citizens alike.

Although these studies differ in their specific analytical focuses, theoretical frameworks and findings, they share a commitment to investigate the idea that democracy requires democrats in order to function. Ordinary citizens are important in facilitating democratization as well as in preserving the integrity of democratic institutions. Well-established democratic values and an engaged citizenry willing to protect them are therefore a crucial asset for democratic survival. Democracy, however, is a contentious idea. Different people understand democracy in different ways, and this diversity has implications for how citizens evaluate the performance of democratic institutions and perceive their legitimacy.

3.2 A Multidimensional Conception of Democracy

Most scholars will agree that a necessary condition for a political regime to be called a 'democracy' is that different parties or candidates compete for the votes of the citizenry in free and fair elections. Today, most countries hold some form of popular elections to select national leaders, but many are implemented within an authoritarian political system, for authoritarian leaders may use elections to consolidate regime legitimacy, gauge the level of regime support or help in political recruitment and selection (Gandhi & Lust-Okar, 2009). The emphasis is therefore on 'free and fair', meaning that elections should be the culmination of a political process in which multi-party competition occurs on an even field, electoral institutions are transparent, and the media provide reliable information to citizens.

Although the idea that free and fair elections are a condition *sine qua non* for democracy is not controversial, a long-standing debate has surrounded the question of whether elections should be considered as a mere necessary condition for democratic rule, or if in fact their presence is sufficient to characterize a political regime as a democracy. Several authors, such as Schumpeter (1942) and Przeworski et al. (2000), have proposed a 'minimalist' idea of democracy in which this electoral dimension is the only essential one. From this perspective, more 'maximalist' conceptualizations risk including more contentious dimensions that can compromise theory development and empirical analysis.

Many others, by contrast, have argued that minimalist definitions can omit crucial components, thereby limiting their validity (Munck & Verkuilen, 2002).

Today, most scholars of democracy acknowledge that this concept is complex and multidimensional (Huber et al., 1997), although there is no consensus as to how many dimensions this concept should include, let alone on what exactly the substance of such dimensions should be. For example, one of the leading sources for empirical analysis of democracy, the V-DEM project (Lindberg et al., 2014), distinguishes between the seven dimensions mentioned above, namely electoral, liberal, majoritarian, consensual, participatory, deliberative, and egalitarian. Other analyses include a smaller number of dimensions, often three or four (Dalton et al., 2007; Norris, 2011; Welzel, 2013), whereas others distinguish only between *procedural* and *substantive* understandings of democracy, as democracy may be defined either in terms of specific formal rules and institutions or in terms of the outcomes that it produces (Munck, 2016). Still others further expand multidimensional conceptualizations to include as many as nine or ten categories (Baviskar & Malone, 2004; Bratton et al., 2005).

A vibrant debate on the nature of democracy is therefore ongoing, and the many typologies and conceptual frameworks proposed by scholars attest to the high degree of diversity in this field. However, to take stock of this broad scholarship or discuss the merits and limitations of the various conceptualizations would transcend the scope of this manuscript. In choosing our theoretical framework, we needed to identify a limited number of dimensions that would resonate with comparative research and at the same time be suitable for the context of Southeast Asia, the region we focus on in this Element. We have thus decided to ground our analysis in a distinction among three main dimensions of democracy that have received special attention in research based on public opinion surveys (Ulbricht, 2018) and that, based on our previous research and the history of the region discussed in the next section, should resonate in the Southeast Asian context.[9]

The first dimension of democracy we focus on is the *liberal* one, sometimes also known as *pluralist*. This variant, which emphasizes limits on elected governments and on the principles of individual rights (Fawcett, 2018), is

---

[9] To be sure, given the historical profile of democratic development in the region discussed in the previous section, an additional dimension worth exploring could be the deliberative one. There are two reasons, however, why we opted against including it in our analysis. First, in a previous pilot study based on the Indonesian case (Fossati & Martinez i Coma, 2020), we found that this dimension did not have much discriminatory power by itself (i.e., the loading factors were very low, especially when compared with the other dimensions, showing that the items that create the deliberative dimension did not add much to the analysis). Second and relatedly, when running the pilot, we observed that the deliberative dimension was the least differentiated, as it overlapped with other dimensions such as the liberal and egalitarian.

often described as an especially important dimension of democracy given that, as discussed above, scholars of comparative politics distinguish between electoral and liberal democratic regimes. Liberalism is of course a broad concept in itself, but within the context of research on conceptions of democracy, liberal understandings of democracy typically stress individual freedoms, civil and political rights, and equal justice before the law (Diamond, 1999). The implementation of these freedoms and rights is closely intertwined with the protection of various kinds of minorities from possibly illiberal majorities as well as with the establishment of a system of institutional checks and balances that limits the power of the executive, thereby protecting citizens from abuses of power. For many, these characteristics are as essential as free and fair elections in a democratic political system.

Second, participation is a crucial element of democracy. From a *participatory* perspective, voting is important, but greater emphasis is placed on citizens' public engagement in politics through various channels, many of which are informal (Barber, 2003). Participatory politics entails a civically minded, engaged citizenry that exerts its full democratic rights not only by voting, but also by discussing politics in public debates and participating in non-electoral initiatives such as protests, demonstrations and boycotts. Because the notion of participatory democracy rests upon the principle that democracy is government by the people, scholars working from this perspective have been critical of the fact that contemporary democracies rely heavily on representation through intermediary institutions and formal electoral channels. This dimension emphasizes the importance of direct avenues for political participation, such as town meetings, public hearings and citizen assemblies; other mechanisms such as referenda and plebiscites; and engagement through civil society organizations. Although this dimension is often neglected in empirical studies (Munck & Verkuilen, 2002), the idea that public participation beyond elections is crucial for democracy is not new. For example, in his seminal work, Robert Dahl (1973) identifies participation as one of the two key dimensions of democratic politics (the other being competition). A participatory conception of democracy is therefore the second dimension of democracy that we include in our theoretical framework.

Finally, the *egalitarian* or *social* dimension asks whether all citizens are equally empowered. Although democracy may guarantee a wide range of rights and freedoms, as well as plenty of opportunity for political participation, such provisions are meaningless if a substantial share of the population is unable to meet its own basic social needs. In this perspective, inequalities (economic or otherwise) are seen as fatal impediments to the full development and exercise of rights and liberties (Young, 2002). A social perspective on democracy thus probes the fairness of the distribution of material and non-material resources in a society, which are typically addressed with economic and social policies (Huber et al., 1997). This perspective asks, for example, whether citizens are protected from poverty, whether access to basic rights such as education and healthcare is guaranteed for all, and whether people have the same opportunities in life regardless of their social background. In other words, adequate standards of living are a prerequisite for the exercise of democratic freedoms and participation. A social dimension is therefore the third and final understanding of democracy that we analyse in this Element.

It is important to distinguish between these various dimensions in empirical research on democracy. At the macro-level, when we study patterns of democratic development across space and over time, it should be remembered that, although some of those dimensions are closely related and may evolve simultaneously (Coppedge et al., 2011), this is not always the case. For example, political equality may or may not be closely associated with the development of the checks and balances emphasized in the liberal dimension, because the relationship between the two may be contingent on specific historical trajectories in each country. At the micro-level, as we discuss in the next two sections, individuals may hold significantly different ideas of what it means to be a democracy. This indicates that ordinary citizens may have divergent – and possibly conflicting – normative values about what a democracy is supposed to deliver (Ulbricht, 2018), which in turn may have repercussions for political behaviour.

3.3 Implications of the Meaning of Democracy

We have already discussed the importance of democratic attitudes – specifically of support for, and satisfaction with, democracy – for democratic consolidation. When democratic legitimacy falters, democracies are exposed to the risk of authoritarian reversals, as citizens will be less likely to appreciate the value of democratic rule and preserve it against its authoritarian alternatives. Although establishing the nexus between democratic attitudes and regime outcomes has proved challenging in empirical research (Claassen, 2020), the idea that democratic values or 'culture' have implications for macro-level institutional change is well established in the literature. It is only more recently, however, that scholars have begun to fully analyse the implications of heterogeneity in conceptions of democracy among individuals. Even when we can identify patterns of similarity and differences between countries in their respective citizens' prevailing understandings of democracy, a substantial level of within-country heterogeneity persists in most societies. In any political community, people differ greatly in how they conceptualize democracy. What are, then, the repercussions of such differences for other important attitudinal orientations and for political behaviour?

A first strand of the literature has observed that citizens vary not only in the substantive meaning they attribute to democracy, but also in the complexity of their conceptions of democracy. When responding to open-ended questions, most people do have a clear idea of what democracy means, even in non-Western settings or least-developed countries. Yet most of them will be able to identify only one dimension of democracy, while only a minority will mention two or more dimensions (Canache, 2012; Shin & Kim, 2018). Such differences in cognitive sophistication are important for democratic attitudes, especially self-reported support for democracy. Research from several world regions, including Latin America (Baviskar & Malone, 2004; Canache, 2012), Africa (Mattes & Bratton, 2007) and cross-regional studies (Cho, 2014), has shown that individuals who have a more sophisticated, multidimensional conception of democracy are more likely to support democratic rule. An important contribution of these studies is to have identified the role of political knowledge and sophistication in shaping patterns of democratic legitimacy, thereby further demonstrating the usefulness of studying various dimensions of democracy in scholarly research.

More recent work has embraced the idea of democracy as a complex, multi-dimensional concept, and has sought to uncover relationships between specific understandings of democracy and other political attitudes and behaviours. Some of this research has maintained the focus on support for democracy as a key dependent variable. Canache (2012), for example, has found with Latin American samples that support for democracy is substantially higher among individuals who see democracy as a matter of individual freedoms, as opposed to other features such as economic and social outcomes. Other scholars have instead studied the implications of conceptions of democracy for democratic satisfaction and legitimacy. Given that democratic legitimacy, like that of any regime (Gilley, 2006), is tied to 'performance', having different ideas of what democracy is about should generate different expectations about what exactly democracy is supposed to deliver. Citizens' evaluations of democratic performance could thus be a function of their conceptions of democracy, and indeed some studies have corroborated this argument. In Europe, citizens who have 'higher ideals' about democracy (i.e., they identify several aspects as being 'very important' for democracy) display overall lower levels of trust in democratic institutions; in East Asia, citizens with a liberal idea of democracy are significantly less satisfied with, or supportive of, their country's political regime (Huang et al., 2013; Zhai, 2019). Finally, some scholars have focused more specifically on participatory understandings of democracy, uncovering a strong link between this idea of participatory democracy and patterns of political participation (Bengtsson & Christensen, 2016; Canache, 2012; Gherghina & Geissel, 2017).

Again, these empirical studies show that conceptions of democracy matter beyond concept formation, because they have observable implications for how citizens evaluate democracy and engage in democratic life. This literature, however, still focuses overwhelmingly on Western societies and Latin America; although Southeast Asian countries are often included in regional and cross-regional analyses of aggregate-level data, we still know little of the micro-level drivers and the implications of conceptions of democracy in this region.

3.4 Research Design

As indicated earlier, our analysis of the meaning of democracy in Southeast Asia is based on an original survey that we have implemented in the five countries of Indonesia, Malaysia, the Philippines, Singapore and Thailand. To collect data, we have used a web-based platform set up by an international survey research company. In cooperation with local contractors in the five countries, respondents were recruited with the help of modest material incentives. Between October and December 2020, potential respondents were sent a link through which they could access the questionnaire, and about 1,200 responses were collected in each country, for a total of 6,128 responses. The welcome page of the survey questionnaire contained detailed information about the scope of the research project and researchers' contact information.[10] It further informed potential respondents that their participation was voluntary and, as assessed by the investigators, entailed no risks for the participant. Confidentiality was assured by the fact that survey responses were collected anonymously, as participants were not asked to disclose any information that could allow the contractor or the researchers to identify them. The resulting pool of participants, as documented in the online appendix (Table 1), shows remarkable diversity in demographic and socioeconomic background.

The use of online surveys with respondents recruited from existing panels or pools of volunteers/workers presents strengths and limitations that are worth a brief discussion. On the one hand, the sampling strategy in online survey research is typically non-random, which creates well-known issues of self-

---

[10] Respondents could choose to take the surveys in one of the local languages in which the instrument was translated (Bahasa Indonesia for Indonesia, Malay for Malaysia and Singapore, Tagalog for the Philippines and Thai for Thailand) and English.

selection. Furthermore, there may be some specific demographic segments, such as older generations and individuals of lower educational attainment, that may be especially difficult to reach with this methodology. The practical implication of these limitations for our study is that in general, as with any non-random sample, it may be difficult to draw descriptive inferences regarding the populations from which these samples are drawn (Baker et al., 2013). For example, we would not be able to conclude with confidence that, say, 30% of Thai people subscribe to a liberal view of democracy, while 35% hold an egalitarian conception. For this reason, will refrain from drawing such types of inferences in this Element.

On the other hand, however, web-based surveys are widely used and trusted to make inferences regarding relationships between variables, which is our primary goal. In studying popular conceptions of democracy, we are interested in whether and how various dimensions of a complex attitudinal construct are coherently understood, how they relate with one another, and what empirical associations they have with other attitudinal and behavioural variables. The use of web-based surveys for similar purposes has grown exponentially in recent years, as web-based platforms facilitate collecting data from samples that behave very similarly to those randomly selected from population frames. A growing body of research has compared data from online panels and market-places such as Amazon's MTurk with data from general populations, suggesting that concerns about the external validity of online samples are exaggerated (Berinsky et al., 2012). In the specific context of research on political ideology, previous research has suggested that findings regarding relationships between variables are virtually identical across samples collected online and in face-to-face interviews (Clifford et al., 2015).

This literature, therefore, reassures us that online samples are generally less different from the general population than commonly thought. A legitimate concern, however, is that internet penetration and access could be a limiting factor to consider when implementing online surveys in the context of low and middle-income countries. According to World Bank data, the percentage of population individuals using the internet ranges from a minimum of 47% in the Philippines and 54% in Indonesia, to 76% in Singapore, 78% in Thailand and 90% in Malaysia.[11] While this invites caution in interpreting the findings, it should be noted that online surveys have been used extensively in the countries under assessment to analyse various social and political issues, from perceived threat of crime in the Philippines (Maxwell, 2019) to partici-pation inequality in Thailand (Sinpeng, 2017) and perceptions of COVID-19

---

[11] https://data.worldbank.org/indicator/IT.NET.USER.ZS, consulted 15 February 2022.

in Indonesia (Harapan et al., 2020), just to mention a few examples. Furthermore, to enhance our samples' representativeness of the general populations, we placed sample quotas on age, gender, region (country-specific), religion and education. To facilitate self-administration among various population segments, we made the survey questionnaire easily accessible from personal devices such as smartphones and tablets, which have the advantage of being flexible and adapt to respondents' times constraints. As with most samples collected online, ours is biased in favour of males and younger, better-educated respondents, as detailed in Table 1 in the Appendix. However, despite these discrepancies between sample and general population, the sufficiently large sample sizes ensure that many responses were collected even for such under-represented population segments, so that the regression analysis we perform in the next section can include these socioeconomic and demographic covariates.

We asked respondents about their views on a wide range of social and political issues, the most important being what they understand by 'democracy'. As discussed in the first section, the rationale of focusing on public understandings of democracy – as opposed to measuring support for democracy as a political regime – is that, given the almost universally positive connotation of the word 'democracy' as well as the contested meaning of the term, general questions about support for democracy may not generate meaningful responses (Dalton, 1994). To be sure, our questionnaire does include questions that allow us to gauge self-reported support for democracy, and in the next section we analyse the relationship between conceptions of democracy and support for democracy. But when measuring understandings of democracy, the issue of the desirability bias associated with the 'D-word', which many scholars have discussed, is less pressing. Instead of asking one of the various questions about how desirable democracy is, we simply ask what features the respondent sees as being important for a democracy. As observed by Ulbricht (2018), this question relates to broad normative orientations that are contentious, as it is hard to rank the various dimensions of democracy in terms of their desirability. The pro-democracy normative bias is therefore not a methodological challenge here, as there is no clear 'right answer' that respondents may feel induced to choose (Seligson, 2004).

The challenge in measuring understandings of democracy is, first, to develop an operationalization that accounts for the complexity of the concept, while at the same time being easy to understand for the ordinary citizens who participate in the survey. Our conceptualization of democracy treats it as a latent and multidimensional concept. By 'latent' we mean that it is not directly observable; we can gather individuals' understandings via multiple observed variables. The survey questions used to generate these variables should mirror the conceptual

Table 2 The twenty items measuring four dimensions of democracy

Dimension	Item
Electoral	All adult citizens have the right to vote in elections
Electoral	Elections are free from fraud or vote-buying
Electoral	Elections are free from intimidation or violence
Electoral	Elections are fair for all political parties.
Electoral	Governments are punished in elections when they have done a bad job
Liberal	Citizens have the right to own property
Liberal	The courts can stop the government if it acts against the constitution
Liberal	Citizens have the right to choose and profess any religion
Liberal	Citizens have the same rights regardless of their race and ethnicity
Liberal	Men and women have equal rights
Egalitarian	Government policies help reduce the difference between the rich and the poor
Egalitarian	Access to basic education and healthcare is guaranteed for all
Egalitarian	The government protects all citizens against poverty
Egalitarian	The government ensures law and order for all
Egalitarian	Public goods such as roads and other infrastructure are provided
Participatory	People are free to discuss politics in public, demonstrate and protest
Participatory	People participate in politics and civic life beyond elections
Participatory	Voters discuss politics with people they know before deciding how to vote
Participatory	Opposition parties are free to operate, criticize the government and run for elections
Participatory	Women participate in politics as much as men do

framework and be as easy to understand and as unambiguous as possible for survey respondents. By 'multidimensional' we mean that understandings of democracy may vary, as there are electoral, liberal, egalitarian and participatory characteristics that define this concept. Part of valid measurement is the proper alignment of the theoretical dimensions of democracy with its empirical instrument, and the survey questions therefore must exhaustively cover all these dimensions.

Table 2 reports the twenty items we have designed to capture the latency and multidimensionality of the concept and to allow a thorough empirical investigation of public understandings of democracy. As the table shows, we cover the electoral, liberal, egalitarian and participatory dimensions of democracy with five statement each, for a total of twenty. The statements are intended to cover the relevant features of each dimension. Hence, the statements on the electoral dimension statements capture democratic procedural features such as universal suffrage and electoral integrity; the liberal items refer to individual freedoms as well as institutional checks and balances; for the egalitarian dimension, the statements touch upon themes such as social insurance and inequality; finally, the participatory dimension items mostly capture informal aspects of political participation.

The various dimensions of democracy are therefore disaggregated into easily understandable items that we ask survey participants to respond to. To ensure that respondent attention remains high throughout this relatively long list of twenty items, we present it to our participants in five separate matrix questions, each containing only one item from each of the four dimensions. More precisely, each question asks:

> *People disagree about what is important for a country to be a democracy. Below you find a list of 4 features that might be considered as being important for democracy. Please indicate how important you think each of the following features is for being a democracy by using a scale in which 1 means 'not important at all' and 10 means 'extremely important'.*

This setup not only helps break down the task into shorter, more manageable questions, but also mitigates the risk of 'straight lining' responses for related items belonging to the same dimension of democracy. The four items in each matrix question, as they represent the four different dimensions of democracy, are rather different substantively. Furthermore, to prevent biases related to ordering, we have randomized the item order in each matrix question, as well as the order in which the five questions are presented.

A second challenge in designing items to measure public understandings of democracy is that the sub-indexes for the various dimensions identified should have sufficient levels of internal consistency. For one, although the theoretical literature has offered clear (if contested) definitions of what concepts such as 'liberal' or 'egalitarian' may mean, the extent to which each of these dimensions resonates in mass publics as a coherent construct is an open question. Second, as suggested by Chu and Huang (2010, p. 121) in their study of democratic attitudes in Asia, the meaning of such terms may be context-specific. Popular conceptions of democracy may have been so contaminated by competing public discourses that the word 'democracy' may have lost much of its conceptual clarity and semantic consistency. Our strategy to address this issue is to disaggregate the concept of democracy into various dimensions and into multiple, specifically worded items that leave little room for interpretation. Yet still, the extent to which, say, a 'liberal' idea of democracy resonates in the same way across borders is an empirical question that needs to be verified.

To test whether the four indexes we have designed are sufficiently reliable as measures of the various dimensions of democracy, we calculate their internal consistency in the five countries surveyed. Specifically, the Cronbach's alpha is a commonly used measure of internal consistency that assumes higher values when a set of items shows high levels of inter-correlation, which indicates that the items indeed behave as a group in measuring a common related factor. The results, reported in Table 3, show that the four indexes are reliable indicators, as they achieve high alpha coefficient values overall in all countries. Although there is some variation across country, the electoral, liberal and egalitarian indexes have Cronbach's values of about .80 or higher, whereas values for the participatory dimension are somewhat lower. These results reassure us that the scales we have designed perform well in measuring the various conceptions of democracy in different political and cultural contexts.

A third element to consider are alternative classifications of some of our items into other dimensions. For example, we classify the item 'Men and women have equal rights' in the liberal dimension, but it could well be categorized under the egalitarian dimension. Likewise, we classify 'Women participate in politics as much as men do' in the participatory dimension, but it would not be problematic to allocate it to the egalitarian. In Section 4.4, we report on a series of robustness checks we have performed to probe the stability of our findings, two of which involve alternative re-classifications of the items into different dimensions. The results, reported in the Appendix, show that our main findings are not sensitive to such reclassifications. Furthermore, there are two reasons that lead us to keep our original specification. First, the Cronbach's alphas for alternative classification options would not be better than the ones displayed in Table 3.[12] Second, the classification in Table 2 provides an even distribution of items for each dimension.

We have therefore developed a new methodological approach that accounts for the multidimensionality of the concept of democracy, the non-exclusivity of the various dimensions and the complexity of each dimension, and we have implemented it with a survey questionnaire that is not exceedingly demanding for respondents. This provides strong foundations for the empirical analysis that we perform in the next section.

---

[12] The classification of the other options as well as their reliability scores is available in the Appendix.

Table 3 Reliability scores for the four indexes of conceptions of democracy

	Electoral	Liberal	Egalitarian	Participatory
Indonesia	.84	.83	.90	.78
Malaysia	.83	.76	.88	.74
Philippines	.75	.79	.85	.74
Singapore	.83	.86	.87	.77
Thailand	.86	.86	.88	.86

4 Structure and Implications of the Meaning of Democracy

In this section, we analyse the micro-level data we have collected to study the structure of popular understandings of democracy in Southeast Asia. We have already discussed how our methodology to measure understandings of the democracy includes the 'necessary' electoral dimension and the three more contentious ideas of democracy included in our conceptual framework, namely the liberal, social-egalitarian and participatory dimensions. Here, we start by analysing some descriptive statistics and correlations among these four indexes, and we then move to regression analysis to identify whether, and to what extent, public conceptions of democracy vary according to socio-demographic factors such as education, income, ethnicity and religion. Again, we focus on identifying overall patterns in the region, but we also perform the analysis separately for each country, which allows a comparative approach to identify areas of convergence and divergence across the five cases. This first analysis of the survey data serves as the foundation for the second part of the section, where we study the implications of liberal, egalitarian and participatory understandings of democracy for other attitudes and political behaviours. The results offer a comprehensive view of how distinct understandings of democracy are linked with social identities, political ideology, regime preferences and political behaviour. A report on a series of robustness checks included in the Appendix concludes the empirical analysis.

4.1 How Do Southeast Asians Understand Democracy?

To what extent do citizens in the five countries we have surveyed understand democracy in electoral, liberal, egalitarian and participatory terms? To answer this question, we can calculate simple arithmetic means of responses to the five items for each index, and we can first use this measure to examine how aggregate scores of understandings of democracy vary by index and by country. The results, reported in Figure 3, indicate similar patterns across the five cases.

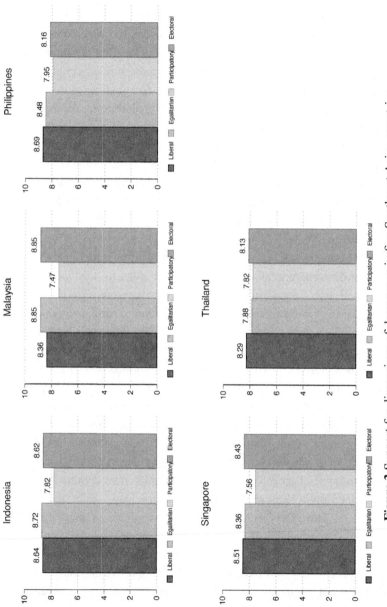

Figure 3 Support for dimensions of democracy in five Southeast Asian countries

First, the electoral dimension, which is considered by scholars as a necessary condition of democratic rule, is indeed widely perceived by respondents in our samples as being essential to democracy, as it scores above 8 in all countries. At the same time, however, the bar charts also show that this dimension does not score especially high when compared with liberal or social–egalitarian conceptions. In all countries, liberal and egalitarian conceptions of democracy have similar (typically, slightly higher) scores compared to the electoral index. Again, given that we are working with non-randomly selected samples, these results should be interpreted cautiously, and they do not allow us to establish conclusively which of the various dimensions is predominant. Yet these data clearly indicate that Southeast Asian citizens have a multidimensional understanding of democracy, as one would expect given the complexity of the concept. We also do not see much evidence that social–egalitarian conceptions of democracy may be more entrenched or popular than liberal ones, as existing research has suggested. Instead, as we further discuss below, a basic electoral understanding of democracy seems to be closely intertwined with liberal and egalitarian ideas.

A second observation is that the participatory dimension is ranked as the least essential for democracy in all five countries. The index for this dimension is below 8 for all cases, ranging from a low of 7.56 in Singapore, a country that we have described as having an especially weak tradition of participatory politics, to a high of 7.95 in the Philippines. Although the difference between the participatory index and the other three may not appear as large, it is statistically significant if a conventional test of means is performed, which shows that participatory items are consistently ranked as less important for democracy than electoral, liberal and egalitarian attributes.[13] These figures resonate with the reliability coefficients shown in Table 3, which were slightly lower for the participatory index. Among the three substantive conceptions of democracy, participatory ideas are somewhat less likely to be understood as a coherent dimension than liberal or egalitarian ones, and citizens on average are less likely to evaluate the various items related to informal participation as being essential for democracy. This, however, should not be interpreted as suggesting that participatory understandings of democracy are less consequential than liberal or social–egalitarian ones. First, even if most Southeast Asians may not subscribe to a participatory view of democracy, this perspective may fully resonate in specific social segments, such as younger cohorts or more educated

---

[13] Paired t-test comparisons for each country between the participatory dimension and its closest dimension (i.e., liberal in Indonesia and Malaysia but egalitarian in the other three countries) show that the values are significantly different from 0 at the .01 level. Thailand is the exception at the .07 level.

Table 4 Correlation coefficients for the four dimensions of democracy
(all countries)

	ELECTORAL	LIBERAL	EGALITARIAN	PARTICIPATORY
ELECTORAL	1.00			
LIBERAL	0.78	1.00		
EGALITARIAN	0.83	0.78	1.00	
PARTICIPATORY	0.68	0.75	0.64	1.00

individuals, as we further analyse in Section 4.2. Second, as we document in the next section, participatory understandings of democracy are in fact linked to several important attitudinal constructs. Results are very similar when relying on alternative classifications of the items in the dimensions.

The data we have presented so far suggest that for most Southeast Asians, democracy is primarily about delivering desirable policy outcomes *and* protecting some key individual rights. Based on the averages reported in Figure 3, we may speculate that the electoral, liberal and egalitarian dimensions of democracy are closely intertwined in the minds of ordinary citizens in the five countries we study. If that is the case, we should observe a high degree of correlation among the three indexes for the dimensions that rank highly based on our participants' responses, namely electoral, liberal and egalitarian. The correlation coefficients reported in Table 4, calculated with the pooled data for all countries, show that this is indeed the case, as both the liberal and (especially) the egalitarian index show high levels of correlations with the electoral index. The high coefficient of .78 further shows that the liberal and egalitarian dimensions, although clearly distinct conceptually, are in fact very closely associated. When asked in survey questions to choose one or the other, Southeast Asians may pick their favourite between the two, be it liberal or egalitarian. But these data indicate that most people in the region understand democracy in both liberal and egalitarian terms. The analytical trade-off between the two may be clear, but both areas are seen as equally essential features of democracy.

As for the participatory index, although it is also positively correlated with the other three, correlation coefficients are lower. This is consistent with the bar charts above, which show a significant difference between responses to the participatory items and items for the remaining three dimensions. It also suggests that a participatory understanding of democracy may be present as a distinct, separate idea of democracy among Southeast Asian publics. Public understandings of democracy in Southeast Asia could therefore be described as having a dual structure in most of the countries we study, as we have found in a pilot study of the Indonesian case (Fossati & Martinez i Coma, 2020). The first dimension is the dominant one, endorsed by most citizens and featuring a blend of electoral, liberal and egalitarian elements. The second, an understanding acknowledged and endorsed by a minority of Southeast Asian citizens, emphasizes the importance of informal participation. These findings demonstrate the importance of conceptualizing democracy as a multidimensional construct, and of employing exhaustive operationalizations in empirical analysis. In the next section, we investigate how conceptions of democracy vary across demographic and socio-economic groups in the five countries. For this analysis, as well as for our study of the implications of understandings of democracy, we focus on the three conceptions of liberal, egalitarian and participatory.

4.2 Socio-Economic Determinants of Conceptions of Democracy

In all countries covered in our study, conceptions of democracy vary significantly across individuals, despite the high average values reported in Figure 3. Just to give an example based on the Malaysian case, more than 25% of the sample scores are relatively low-value (i.e., lower than 7.5) in the liberal conception index, whereas about 40% of respondents score 9 or higher. To be sure, in this example – as in most others – only a few respondents obtain low values on the conception of democracy indexes, which is understandable given that all the scale items refer to very important aspects of democratic politics. Yet this degree of variation does suggest that individuals differ in how essential they perceive the various democratic dimensions to be, and it is sufficient to allow investigation of the socio-demographic factors that are associated with this variation.

Existing research indicates that factors such as age, education, economic background and religion may shape how individuals understand democracy. Age could be an important factor for democratic attitudes because cognitive development, life experiences and learning should be conducive to the emergence of more developed and structured political attitudes (Lechler & Sunde, 2019). Older respondents may, therefore, be more likely to have a well-formed conception of democracy of any kind. As for education, there are two channels through which it could affect democratic attitudes. First, individuals with higher educational attainment have better cognitive skills than those with only modest formal education. They should thus be better able to understand the survey questions and formulate coherent views of democracy (Magalhães, 2014). Second, it has long been established that better-educated individuals are more likely to hold liberal attitudes; therefore, they should be more inclined to think of democracy in liberal terms (Feldman & Newcomb, 2020). Economic factors may also impact individuals' understanding of democracy (Ceka & Magalhaes, 2020). Individuals from higher social classes, for example, have been found to be more likely to have understandings of democracy that are supportive of the status quo (i.e., more liberal than low-income individuals in democratic regimes, and less liberal than low-income individuals in authoritarian regimes). Furthermore, we may hypothesize that low-income individuals, being more vulnerable to economic fluctuations and more familiar with the challenges imposed by economic inequalities (Singer, 2011), may more likely to subscribe to an egalitarian view of democracy. Finally, with regard to religion, many researchers have tied the lower levels of democracy in Muslim-majority countries to specific features of Islamic culture and society, such as particularly conservative views among Muslims on religious issues and gender roles (Fish, 2002).

To explore the relevance of these hypotheses in the Southeast Asian context, we perform regression analysis, for which we estimate models where the three conceptions of democracy indexes (liberal, egalitarian, participatory) are the dependent variables. We thus estimate three models for each country, and we include age, gender, education, income, religion and region as socio-demographic variables of interest. We measure age in years, gender with a binary variable (1 for female), and education with a four-tier variable from lowest to highest educational attainment.[14] As for income, instead of asking directly about monthly or yearly income figures, we rely on an indicator that asks respondents to evaluate their own personal financial situation as *very bad*, *bad*, *neither good nor bad*, *good*, or *very good*. This question has the advantage of reducing the number of missing observations, and it generates a direct measure of perceptions of economic conditions.[15] In the models for Indonesia, the Philippines and Thailand, we include a dummy variable to measure whether the respondent is a member of the religious majority (Muslim, Catholic and Buddhist, respectively). For Malaysia and Singapore, where ethnicity is a more salient social identity, we include a categorical variable that describes the respondent as Chinese, Malay, Indian or a member of another ethnic group. To control for variation across region in the five countries, we include fixed effects for regions in each model. Finally, we also control in our models for two psychological factors that may be related to

---

[14] The lowest baseline level is for respondents who have only primary or lower secondary school, the second for some upper secondary/high school, the third for high school diploma and the highest and fourth group for college-educated respondents.

[15] Responses were aggregated into three categories, namely *very bad/bad*, *neutral* and *good/very good*.

various aspects of democratic attitudes, namely interpersonal trust and life satisfaction.[16]

Results of the estimations are reported in tables 2A–2E in the online appendix. In most of the fifteen models reported in the table, age has a positive and statistically significant effect on conceptions of democracy, meaning that older respondents are more likely to consider the various items of the three dimensions as essential for democracy. To provide an example based on the models estimated for Thailand, compared with a twenty-year-old respondent, a fifty-year-old is estimated to score 0.5 points higher on the liberal index, 0.6 points higher on the egalitarian index and 0.4 points higher on the participatory index. This indicates that older individuals may have overall more developed and coherent conceptions of democracy. The differences in conceptions of democracy across different age cohorts, however, are not large, as the modest magnitude of the estimated coefficients suggests. It is also interesting to note that there is no apparent pattern in terms of which specific understanding of democracy is more prevalent in certain cohorts as opposed to others. We may hypothesize, for instance, that younger respondents may be more likely to endorse participatory understandings of democracy, given that younger generations are usually more involved in informal politics, but the data do not support this proposition.

The results for education are strong and consistent across country. College-educated participants are substantially more likely than low-education respondents to identify liberal, egalitarian and participatory elements as crucial for democracy. Consider, for example, the patterns displayed in Figure 4, which is based on the case of the Philippines. Respondents with college education, compared with those who have lower secondary or elementary education, are estimated to score one full point higher on the liberal and the egalitarian dimension, and 1.3 points higher on the participatory index. These results show an important difference across demographic groups, as better-educated respondents appear to be more aware of the complexity and multidimensionality of the concept of democracy. As previous studies have shown, education has important implications for democratic attitudes, as it contributes to knowledge about – and, eventually, support for – democracy (Cho, 2014). Another interesting pattern concerning the relationship between education and conceptions of democracy is that, although education (college education in particular) is

---

[16] Interpersonal trust is measured with a question asking about attitudes towards people in general: Can most people be trusted, or should one be very careful when dealing with people? For life satisfaction, we use a 10-point scale where higher values indicate a higher level of life satisfaction. We include such variables as controls. In other contexts, it has been found that low levels of trust are associated with strong democratic ideals (Hooghe et al., 2017). Life satisfaction has been shown to influence subjective well-being (Owen et al., 2008; Radcliff & Shufeldt, 2016). Likewise, we include it as a control, as self-perception may also play a role in how individuals view democracy.

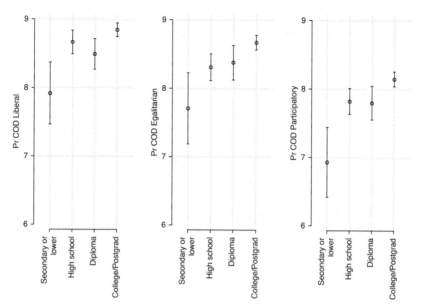

Figure 4 Educational attainment and conceptions of democracy
(the Philippines)

positively and significantly associated with any public understanding of democracy, the link is especially strong for the participatory dimension. In all countries except Thailand, the estimated coefficient for college education is largest for the model with the participatory index than for the other two. Higher education is therefore crucial in developing a multifaceted, comprehensive understanding of democracy, especially with regard to acknowledging and appreciating the importance of informal participation in democratic politics.

The models we estimate also show that income, as measured by a self-assessment of financial conditions, is sometimes associated with conceptions of democracy. The results, however, vary significantly across countries. As mentioned earlier, based on existing research, the expectation is that wealthier people will be supportive of the regime status quo, which means that we should observe lower levels of endorsement of liberal understandings of democracy in authoritarian countries like Malaysia, Singapore and Thailand. Indeed, in both Malaysia and Singapore – but not in Thailand – income is negatively and significantly linked with liberal understandings of democracy, as shown in Figure 5 with an illustration of the Singaporean case.[17] For instance, the

---

[17] The null findings for Thailand could be attributed to the fact that this country's political regimes have long oscillated between democracy and authoritarianism, whereas authoritarian stability has characterized the Singaporean and Malaysian cases.

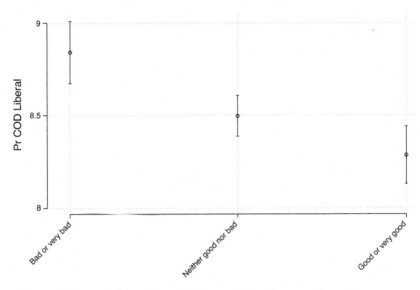

Figure 5 Personal financial conditions and liberal conception of democracy (Singapore)

predicted score on the liberal index in Singapore declines from 8.8 in respondents who evaluate their economic situation as *very bad* or *bad* to 8.3 among those who see their condition as *good* or *very good*. It is also worth noting that in three of the five countries (Indonesia, Malaysia and Singapore) better-off individuals are also less likely to understand democracy in egalitarian terms. Although this relationship is observed only in these three cases (the coefficient is close to zero for Thailand and positive for the Philippines), this pattern suggests that lower-income respondents may be more supportive of the idea that addressing socioeconomic inequalities is a key feature of democracy.

The importance of religious and ethnic identities in shaping popular understandings of democracy varies substantially in the five cases. In the two most homogeneous countries (Thailand and the Philippines), being a member of a religious majority (Buddhist and Catholic, respectively) does not matter for democratic attitudes. However, in the more diverse societies of Indonesia and Malaysia, ethno-religious cleavages do have a bearing on public conceptions of democracy. In Indonesia, Muslims are substantially less likely to understand democracy in liberal terms than religious minorities (on average, they score about 0.5 lower on the liberal index). To be sure, other studies show that there is great heterogeneity among Indonesian Muslims regarding their political ideology, but liberal views are concentrated among religious minorities in this Muslim-majority society (Fossati, 2019).

In Malaysia, where we measure differences across ethnic instead of religious groups, the differences are even more stark, as shown in Figure 6. Muslim Malays are significantly less likely than Chinese Malaysians to believe that the liberal items are essential for democracy (here too, the difference between the two groups is about half a point). Furthermore, the differences between Malays and Chinese are equally important for the two other dimensions, as Malays are more likely to see democracy in egalitarian terms, whereas the Chinese are more likely to endorse participatory understandings of democracy. In this ethnically divided country, citizens of Chinese background (an ethnic and religious minority) are thus significantly more likely to see democracy as a matter of liberal individual rights and political participation, whereas Muslim Malays, the dominant ethnic group, are more likely to associate democracy with material benefits. It is important to appreciate, however, that such large differences among ethnic groups are contingent on the specific historical and political context in each country. Compare, for example, the Malaysian case with that of Singapore, where the same ethnic groups are present. In Singapore, as indicated by the estimated coefficients, no significant differences are observed among ethnic groups, possibly due to the very different path this country has taken in managing inter-ethnic relations. Thus, ideas of democracy may vary substantially across ethnic and religious groups, but whether they do depends on the specific political legacies in each country.

As for the other factors, life satisfaction (as expected) has a strong and positive relationship with the dependent variables in all models, and interpersonal trust (although there is some variation across country and models) is likewise positively related to the three indexes of conceptions of democracy. These associations indicate that more satisfied and more trustful respondents are generally more likely to support the three conceptions of democracy. Finally, region-fixed effects are generally not significant. The exception is Indonesia, where respondents located in the regions of Sumatra, Sulawesi and East Java (all regions with a strong Islamist political tradition) show lower levels of endorsement for liberal and egalitarian understandings of democracy than in other Indonesian regions. Although most of the five cases we study are large countries with substantial subnational diversity in terms of social and cultural make-up, geographical factors do not seem to be driving public conceptions of democracy as significantly as individual ones.

To summarize, the fifteen models we report in appendix tables 2A-2E provide a good overview of the various sociodemographic profiles associated with the various conceptions of democracy. They indicate, first, that better-educated individuals possess a more structured and comprehensive understanding of the various dimensions of democratic politics, and they suggest that other

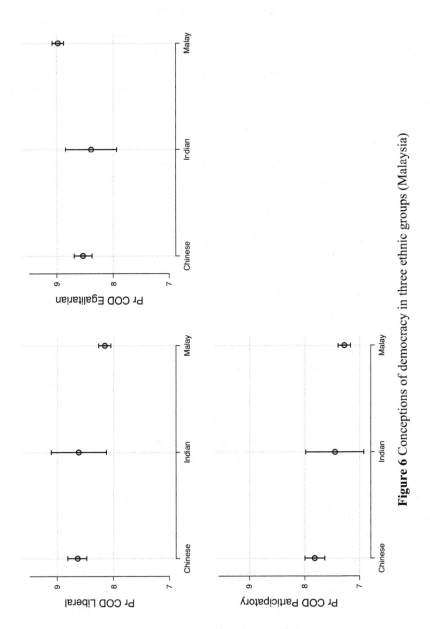

Figure 6 Conceptions of democracy in three ethnic groups (Malaysia)

factors, such as age and income, may also shape public understandings of democracy in some contexts. Second, they point to the importance of social identities such as ethnicity and religion. In the diverse societies of Southeast Asia, ethnic and religious groups often differ in their views of what democracy is about, which indicates that divergent normative preferences may exist between ethnic and religious groups. These differences are plausibly contingent on the historical legacies of state formation that we have discussed above.

4.3 Conceptions of Democracy and Political Behaviour

For the analysis we perform in this section, we build on the premise that conceptions of democracy may have consequences for a wide range of political attitudes and behaviours, and we explore such ramifications following indications from existing research. We focus especially on four main areas. First, we study the relationship between popular understandings of democracy and another key area of democratic attitudes, namely satisfaction with democracy. The general idea we are exploring in these sections is that conceptions of democracy may have consequences for how ordinary people evaluate democratic performance. Second, and related to this, we analyse the association between conceptions of democracy and trust in various institutions, to ascertain whether understandings of democracy underpin different perceptions about the legitimacy of different institutions and of government more generally. Third, we shift our focus to more generalized support for democracy as a political regime. Fourth, we look at the role of ideas of democracy in shaping patterns of political behaviour, especially as it concerns engagement in politics, participation in associational life, and voting.

We employ regression analysis to explore the relationship between conceptions of democracy and important variables in each of these four domains. For each, we start by outlining some theoretical expectations based on the literature reviewed in Section 3 and the specific political context of the five countries. We then briefly describe our approach to conceptualization and measurement, and we present some descriptive statistics on how these variables are distributed in the five samples. Finally, we estimate with the three indexes of conceptions of democracy as independent variables. We discuss how the three conceptions of democracy affect the outcomes of interest and illustrate our findings with examples from the five countries and figures with calculations based on the estimated models.[18]

---

[18] Due to space constraints, we do not report tables with full estimations in the text, but they are all available in the online appendix as indicated below. The discussion of the findings is based on models estimated with all three indexes of conceptions of democracy. Because the three are highly correlated, however, we also provide in the appendix various models estimated with one index at a time. (We thus report four models for each dependent variable and country.)

4.3.1 Satisfaction with Democracy

Conceptions of democracy are foundational to other attitudes such as satisfaction with democracy. The data we have analysed so far suggest that Southeast Asians harbour remarkably diverse views of democracy. The importance of this heterogeneity for democratic satisfaction and legitimacy is that, having different conceptions of democracy, individuals may evaluate democracy by different standards, and thus arrive at different conclusions – for instance, as to how well democracy is performing or whether democratic regimes are the most desirable. Thus, the theoretical framework we adopt here is one in which institutional performance is pivotal to shaping patterns of public support for a regime, be it democratic or otherwise. Yet what exactly is meant by 'performance' may vary across individuals and countries, and it is contingent on the conceptual–normative question of what exactly is meant by the 'D-word'. For example, in a country with very high levels of economic inequality and robust protections for individual freedom, a social–egalitarian democrat may be more inclined to evaluate the state of democracy negatively, whereas a liberal democrat may formulate a more positive evaluation. The process of evaluating democracy is therefore closely tied to the broad, normative orientations that we presented as foundational to the meaning of democracy.

In the context of Southeast Asia, specifically, we have highlighted how liberal understandings of democracy have typically been subordinate to social–egalitarian ones. In political discourse, communitarian ideologies have been prominent, and political elites have often advocated for, and implemented, ideas of democracy in which liberal values and individual freedoms were presented as a threat to social and political stability. The main expectation for empirical analysis is, therefore, that egalitarian democrats will show higher levels of satisfaction with democracy than liberal democrats (i.e. the liberal democracy index should be negatively associated with satisfaction with democracy, while the egalitarian index should be positively associated). As for the participatory index, we have described how participatory traditions vary by country. We should therefore expect that where spaces for informal political participation are especially limited, such as in Singapore, participatory democrats should be more likely to be dissatisfied with democracy. In contrast, this association may not hold in countries that we have described as having stronger participatory legacies.

We use two indicators to measure satisfaction with democracy. The first asks quite simply and directly: 'On the whole, how satisfied or dissatisfied are you with how democracy is practiced in [country]?' Respondents can choose among the categories of *not satisfied at all*, *not very satisfied*, *somewhat satisfied* and *very satisfied*. Only 16.9% of our respondents declare themselves *very satisfied*, while another 47.8% feel *satisfied*, and the remaining 35.3% are either *not very satisfied* (26.3%) or *not satisfied at all* (9%). There is, however, substantial variation in responses across countries. For example, the share of *not satisfied at all* respondents ranges from 5.5% in Singapore to 18.1% in Thailand, while those who are *very satisfied* vary from 12% in Indonesia to 21.5% in Singapore. The second question that we rely on asks respondents to assess whether their country is a democracy; 84.2% in Indonesia, 82.9% in Malaysia, 89.2% in the Philippines, 74.4% in Singapore and 57.9% in Thailand respond to this question affirmatively. Those who believe their country to be a democracy are further asked a second question concerning whether they think the country to be a full democracy, a democracy with minor problems or a democracy with major problems.[19] We combine these two questions into a single indicator, which ranges from the country being perceived as an authoritarian regime (22.7% of responses in all countries) to a full democracy (19.6%).

Tables 3.1A–3.1E in the online appendix report estimations for a set of models in which satisfaction with democracy is the dependent variable.[20] As expected, respondents who score high values in the egalitarian democracy index show systematically higher levels of democratic satisfaction, as the estimated coefficient for the index is positive in all countries and significant in three of the five (the Philippines, Singapore and Thailand). Thus, in Southeast Asia, those who understand democracy as a matter of social and policy outcomes seem to be more satisfied with democracy. As for liberal democrats, they are, as hypothesized, less satisfied with democracy, but only in some countries. Although the liberal democracy index is negatively signed in almost all countries, it is only significant at the .05 level in Indonesia and the Philippines. Somewhat surprisingly, then, those with a strong liberal conception of democracy in countries with a poorly consolidated liberal political culture, such as Singapore and Malaysia, do not seem to be more dissatisfied with democracy than those for whom the liberal dimension is a less essential aspect of democracy. As for the participatory dimension, here too we see a generally negative relationship with satisfaction with democracy, although one that varies by country. The strongest associations between participatory understanding of democracy and lower levels of satisfaction is observed in Singapore and Thailand; in Malaysia, the

---

[19] Admittedly, given the multidimensionality of the idea of democracy that we endorse in this Element, a question that simply asks how 'full' a democracy a certain country may be considered as ambiguous. But in this case, having a question in which the choices can be ordinally ranked is necessary to explore the hypotheses outlined in the previous paragraph.

[20] Given the low number of not satisfied at all respondents in some countries, we recode this variable into a three-category indicator where the two lowest levels of satisfaction are collapsed.

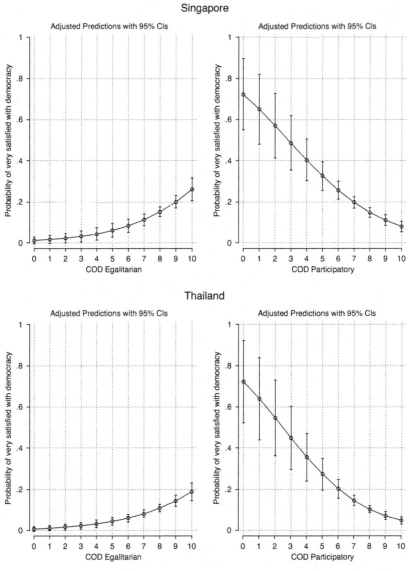

Figure 7 Conceptions of and satisfaction with democracy
(Singapore and Thailand)

coefficient is also negative and significant, whereas it is positive in Indonesia and close to zero in the Philippines.

Thus, the overall pattern emerging from this analysis is that social–egalitarian democrats are significantly more likely to be satisfied with democracy than liberal–participatory democrats in the five countries we study. To illustrate these findings, consider the cases of Singapore and Thailand, represented in Figure 7.

As per the descriptive statistics reported above, these two countries are quite different in terms of democratic satisfaction, as they have, respectively, the highest and lowest levels of satisfaction with democracy in our sample. Nevertheless, as shown below, these two cases display similar patterns in the relationship between conceptions of, and satisfaction with, democracy. In both countries, satisfaction with democracy grows with higher levels of egalitarian conceptions and declines with higher levels of participatory conceptions of democracy. For example, in Thailand, the estimated probability of being very satisfied with democracy, displayed in Figure 7, ranges from 1 to 4% among those who score low (between 1 and 5) on the egalitarian index to about 15% and over above in those who score higher (9 and 10). In contrast, the same probability decreases from values above 40% among those who score low on the participatory index to less than 10% in those who score highest. In Singapore, the relationship is similar: as respondents move to higher values in the participatory index, the probability of being very satisfied with democracy declines from almost 80% to values lower than 20% at participatory values of 9 and higher. The opposite is the case for the egalitarian dimension, and while respondents show negligible probabilities of being very satisfied with democracy at lower values of the egalitarian dimension, the probabilities of being very satisfied increase to over 20% at the highest values.

The models based on the second variable we explore in this section, namely the assessment of a respondent country's political regime, are reported in tables 3.2. A–3.2.E in the online appendix. The results closely mirror those discussed above for satisfaction with democracy, with the egalitarian index positively and significantly associated with the probability of evaluating a country as a democracy in all countries except Malaysia, and liberal and participatory indexes generally being negatively signed and significant at the .05 level in some countries. As an example, the case of the Philippines is represented in Figure 8, which shows expected probabilities to evaluate this country as a *full democracy* given specific values of the egalitarian and liberal democracy indexes. As the figure shows, the expected probability of a positive evaluation of the political regime in the Philippines is higher among those who score high in the egalitarian democracy index or low in the liberal democracy index. This example, as well as the results for the models estimated for the other four cases, further corroborates the argument that popular understandings of democracy have important implications for how ordinary citizens evaluate democracy in their country.

4.3.2 Trust in Institutions

The data we have analysed above indicate that conceptions of democracy shape how ordinary people assess the performance of democratic institutions.

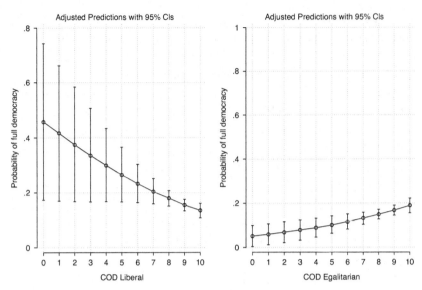

Figure 8 Conceptions of democracy and assessment of political regime (Philippines)

An implication of this finding is that we should also observe a strong connection between popular understandings of democracy and trust in public institutions. Political trust, generally understood as citizens' confidence in government institutions, has long been studied as a key component of government legitimacy, and many researchers have observed that public levels of trust are not unconditional, but rather are influenced by perceptions of institutional performance.[21] Our expectations about the empirical link between conceptions of democracy and trust in institutions are therefore in accordance with what we have outlined above for satisfaction with democracy. Given the political context of the five countries, we should observe a positive relationship between trust and egalitarian understandings of democracy, whereas liberal and participatory democrats should exhibit lower levels of institutional trust.

We have asked our survey participants several questions on how much, if at all, they trust some of the public institutions in their country. The key variable measures overall trust in the national government, which respondents are asked to evaluate on a scale ranging from 1 (*don't trust at all*) to 10 (*trust a great deal*). Responses show a high level of variation across individuals on this question, with almost 30% of respondents choosing values of 5 or lower. The overall average value for this variable is 6.6, and country averages range from Thailand's 5.4 to Singapore's 7.2. In addition to this general question, we elicit

---

[21]　See for instance Van de Walle and Bouckaert (2003) and Thomassen et al. (2017).

expressions of trust for various important institutions and groups, namely local government, political parties, the parliament, courts, the police, the army, the media, business corporations, religious leaders, and scientific experts. Responses to some of these questions, such as those regarding the courts, the police or parliament, are highly correlated (above 0.70) with trust in national government, whereas for other (questions on business, media and religious leaders) the correlation coefficients, although positive, are somewhat lower (slightly below 0.50).

Tables 3.3A–3.3E in the online appendix report the results of linear regression analysis for models in which the dependent variable is trust in the national government. As expected, the coefficient for the egalitarian conception index is positively signed and significant at the .05 level in all countries, which indicates that trust in government is indeed higher among respondents with a social–egalitarian understanding of democracy. The effect of the other two conceptions of democracy, however, varies significantly by country. Participatory understandings of democracy are generally negatively associated with trust in government, especially in the case of Singapore and Thailand, which is consistent with the patterns discussed in the previous section. Indonesia, however, is an exception in this regard, as Indonesians with a higher participatory understanding of democracy are *more*, not less, likely to trust the government. This may be due to the exceptionally high levels of civic and political participation in Indonesia, a feature of this country's politics that sets it apart from many other young democracies (Lussier & Fish, 2012). The more vibrant associational life in Indonesia may be linked to higher levels of institutional trust, especially among individuals who value participation as a key aspect of democratic politics. As for the liberal dimension, the estimated coefficient is negatively signed in all countries except Singapore, but it is only significant at a conventional level in the case of Thailand. Therefore, patterns of political trust in the five countries appear to be following quite closely what we have found for satisfaction with democracy, featuring a general positive association between egalitarian ideas of democracy and trust, as well as some country-specific associations.

To further probe the findings, we have re-estimated the models with the various institution-specific trust questions listed above. The results are generally congruent with those for trust in the national government, as many of these indicators are closely correlated. Nevertheless, it may be worth focusing on some specific results to emphasize points of similarity and divergence across countries. For example, Figure 9 plots curves of estimated trust in the army at various levels of egalitarian and participatory conceptions of democracy in Indonesia and Thailand, where the armed forces have played an important

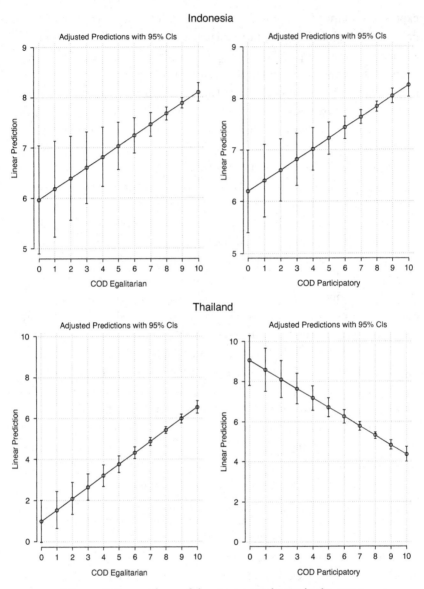

Figure 9 Conceptions of democracy and trust in the army
(Indonesia and Thailand)

political role.[22] In both cases, egalitarian ideas of democracy are positively linked with trust in the army. For instance, estimated trust in the army in Indonesia increases from 7 to 8.1 when moving from a value of 5 to 10 in the egalitarian democracy index, and the increase is even greater in Thailand

---

[22] The full results are reported in tables 3.4.A–3.4.E of the online appendix.

(from 4 to 6 in the same range). As for participatory conceptions of democracy, the military, both historically and at present, has played a prominent role in the suppression of contentious politics in both countries, so it seems warranted to expect a negative relationship between participatory understandings of democracy and trust in the army in both cases. Yet such a negative link is only observed in Thailand, while the relation is positive and significant in Indonesia.[23] It is challenging to account for this surprising finding, but perhaps the very high levels of trust for the army among Indonesians, which are partly due to the crucial role played by the armed forces in the highly mobilizing National Revolution, may explain the contrast with Thailand, where perceptions of the army are much more polarized. This illustration reminds us how important it is to consider a country's historical and political context when analysing the relationship between public understanding of democracy and other attitudinal and behavioural variables.

4.3.3 Support for Democracy

As scholars have long recognized, support for a certain political regime can be measured at different levels (Easton, 1975). In the previous two sections, we focused on attitudes regarding how democracy is practiced in a given country and at a given time, and we found that public understandings of democracy have important implications for how citizens evaluate democracy's performance. Although people may be dissatisfied with how democracy works in a specific context, they may remain committed to democracy as a political regime, as they share the ideals and the principles that underpin democratic rule. Norris (2017), to name one example, distinguishes between highly 'specific' political support, such as approval rates for certain prominent office-holders, and more 'diffuse' (and, usually, more stable) support for ideals and principles. The indicators of democratic satisfaction/performance and institutional trust analysed above, for instance, fall between these two extremes. We now turn our attention to a more diffuse level of support for democracy, which we understand as a belief in democracy as the most desirable political system and a rejection of its authoritarian alternatives.

The connection between conceptions of democracy and support for democracy as such understood is less straightforward than the evaluations of democratic performance. Although evaluations of regime performance are contingent on what exactly is being meant by 'democracy', one could be a committed

---

[23] In Indonesia, when the respondent changes from a 5 to a 10 in the participatory COD, trust in the army increases from 7.2 to 8.2. In contrast, in Thailand, the trend is the opposite. When the respondent changes from a 5 to a 10 in the participatory COD, trust in the army shifts from 6.7 to 4.3.

democrat regardless of their liberal, egalitarian or participatory normative preference. For this reason, we do not have strong theoretical expectations about the association between conceptions of democracy and support for democracy. However, it could be that, as mentioned in the previous section when discussing the effect of education on democratic attitudes, those with more structured understandings of democracy of any kind may be more supportive of democratic rule. Furthermore, analysing empirical associations between support for democracy and the three indexes is interesting in itself, as it can reveal whether citizens with a specific conception of democracy are more likely to see themselves as supporters of democracy.

To measure support for democracy, we adopt two binary indicators built from a matrix of four questions that asks respondents to evaluate the desirability of four features of a political regime: (i) to have a democratic political system, (ii) to have a leader who doesn't have to bother with elections and parliament, (iii) to have the army rule, and (iv) to have experts, rather than government, make decisions according to what they think is best for the country. For each question, survey participants assess the desirability of the regime feature as *very bad*, *bad*, *good* or *very good*. The first variable we use simply tracks responses to the question on having a democratic political system, which we recode as a dummy variable (*bad/ very bad* vs. *good/very good*). By this raw measure, our respondents are overwhelmingly (86.5%) in favour of democratic rule, the highest value being observed among the Singaporeans in our sample (90.3%) and the lowest among Thais (76.4%). These figures are consistent with previous findings in the literature, which have identified high levels of popular support for democracy in most world regions.

Nevertheless, a respondent who professes support for democracy may misunderstand the concept, combining a vague, normative commitment to democracy with support for various forms of authoritarianism. We therefore build a second, more demanding indicator that not only tracks self-reported support for democracy, but also conveys rejection of the three authoritarian features of political regimes listed in the matrix question. By this measure, a respondent is classified as a 'genuine' democrat if they state that they support democracy *and* reject rule by the army, rule by experts and rule by unaccountable strong leaders. This stronger requirement dramatically reduces the number of democrats in our sample, as only 11.3% of respondents support democracy and reject the three authoritarian regime features. The highest share of respondents who support and understand democracy is found in the samples for Thailand and Singapore (both at 21%), while in the remaining three countries, the share of genuine democrats is much lower in Malaysia (9.7%), and abysmal in Indonesia and the Philippines (4.3% and 2.7%, respectively).

Tables 3.5.A–3.5.E in the online appendix report the results of a series of logit models in which the outcome variable is the binary indicator of self-reported support for democracy. The table shows a strong pattern with remarkable consistency across cases: in all countries, the estimated coefficient for the liberal conception index is positive and significant at least at the .05 level. In contrast, signs and significance of the coefficients for egalitarian and participatory understandings of democracy are inconsistent across model specification and country. Liberal democrats are therefore substantially more likely to identify themselves as supporters of democracy than those who do not perceive liberal aspects as being essential features of democratic rule. For example, when moving towards higher levels of the liberal democracy index (from a value of 5 to 10), the estimated probability of describing a democratic political system as *good* or *very good* increases by 21 percentage points in Indonesia, 10 points in Malaysia, 34 points in the Philippines, 26 points in Singapore and 16 points for Thailand. Figure 10 illustrates this finding by showing the estimated probability of supporting democracy at various levels of liberal conceptions of democracy, as measured by our index, in the Philippines and Singapore, and it shows that the relationship is strong and positive in both countries. These findings indicate that individuals with a strong conception of liberal democracy are most likely to appreciate and value democracy. They offer an interesting contrast with the findings we have reported for satisfaction with democracy, as liberal democrats

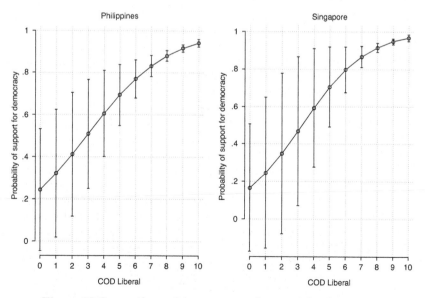

Figure 10 Conceptions of democracy and support for democracy
(the Philippines and Singapore)

tend to be quite critical of how democracy works in their country. Having a clear idea of democracy as a liberal political regime may therefore be associated with higher levels of dissatisfaction with democracy *and* higher levels of support for democracy as a political regime.

The models estimated with the more demanding binary indicator that identifies 'genuine' democrats, reported in tables 3.6.A–3.6.E of the online appendix, paint a picture similar to those with self-reported support for democracy. Because of the very low numbers of genuine democrats in Indonesia, Malaysia and the Philippines, in Figure 11 we estimate the models for Singapore and Thailand alone. In both countries, we find that the coefficient for the liberal conception index is large in magnitude, positively signed and significant. Adopting a more stringent criterion to identify an individual as a democrat, therefore, dramatically changes the number of democrats in a given population (in our case, in the five samples we have collected). At the same time, however, this different operationalization does not change the association we have uncovered between liberalism and support for democracy as a political regime. We further discuss this finding in the conclusions.

4.3.4 Participation

In the previous sections, we have documented a strong association between conceptions of democracy and other attitudes, showing the importance of understandings of democracy for democratic satisfaction and the legitimacy

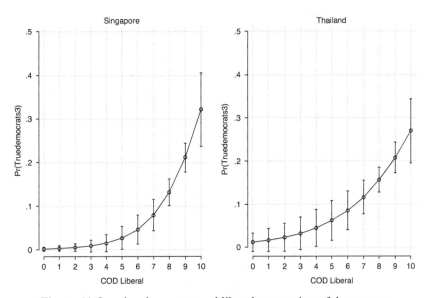

Figure 11 Genuine democrats and liberal conception of democracy
(Singapore and Thailand)

of democratic institutions. Ideas about the meaning of democracy, however, may be consequential not only for other political attitudes, but for political behaviour as well. A useful starting point is to think of understandings of democracy as a proxy for political sophistication. Individuals with a more complex and articulate understanding of democracy should be more aware of formal and informal avenues for political participation, and may therefore be more likely to engage in various political activities (Canache, 2012). From this perspective, conceptions of democracy may function in a similar way as a 'resource' that facilitates political participation (Brady et al., 1995), and we should therefore expect that any idea of democracy may be associated with higher levels of participation.

But beyond this general association, specific understandings of democracy may be tied to certain forms of political behaviour, as demonstrated in existing research. On the one hand, when political participation – especially informal participation – is appreciated as an essential component of democratic politics, behaviour should follow suit. Some studies on European samples, for example, have revealed a connection between participatory understandings of democracy and participation, as individuals with a well-defined participatory idea of democracy are more likely to engage in informal activities of political partici-pation (Bengtsson & Christensen, 2016; Gherghina & Geissel, 2017). On the other hand, as observed by Canache (2012, p. 1138), individuals with a liberal understanding of democracy may be less likely to engage in informal politics and more likely to participate in politics through formal institutional channels such as voting. Therefore, our expectation is that individuals with a strong participatory conception of democracy will be more likely to participate in politics, especially through informal channels, whereas for liberal democrats, participation is less likely to take place through informal avenues.

We adopt three variables to measure informal and formal political participa-tion. The first is a straightforward question asking how interested respondents are in politics. Overall, our sample displays fairly high levels of political interest, with only 41.2% of respondents saying that they are *not interested at all* or *not very interested* in politics, and the remaining 58.8% being *somewhat interested* or *very interested*. Respondents in Thailand and the Philippines appear especially engaged (in both countries, more than 20% of respondents describe themselves as *very interested* in political matters), while Indonesia has the largest share of participants (15.6%) who say that they are *not interested at all* in politics. Second, we leverage self-reported data on membership in various types of associations (cultural/educational, religious, humanitarian/charitable, political, environmental, professional). Following existing research (Howard & Gilbert, 2008), we build an index that counts the number of associations of which the respondent is an active or non-active member, and we obtain a variable of participation in associational life ranging from 0 to 12.[24] About half of respondents in the five samples report fairly low levels of informal participation (0–3), while 23.9% are more engaged individuals with high scores ranging from 8–12. In terms of variation across country, the lowest median value is recorded in Singapore (2) and the highest in the Philippines (5). Finally, our third measure of political participation concerns formal participation through voting; it is based on a question asking respondents if they voted in the last general elections. Although self-reported measures of voting often suffer from overreporting or inaccurate recall, the figures we obtain from this question are not far from official turnout figures in the relevant elections.[25]

Results for ordered logit models where political interest is the dependent variable are reported in tables 3.7.A–3.7.E of the online appendix and show a strong and consistent association between political interest and participatory understandings of democracy. In all countries, the estimated coefficient for the participatory conception index is positive and significant, showing that individuals who understand democracy in participatory terms are more likely to report being interested in political issues. For example, an Indonesian scoring 10 in the participatory democracy index is estimated to be about 12 percentage points more likely to be *very interested* in politics than one scoring 5, while this difference is of 13 percentage points in Malaysia, 6 in the Philippines, 18 in Singapore and 21 in Thailand. This is a first piece of evidence in support of the argument that participatory democrats exhibit higher levels of informal political engagement in the five samples we have collected. Participatory democrats are more likely to be interested in politics, and, plausibly, to spend the time and make the efforts that are needed to acquire sufficient information to keep elected officials accountable. We find no evidence, however, of a connection between political interest and either egalitarian or liberal conceptions of democracy, as estimated coefficients for these two indexes are inconsistent across models.

When we focus on engagement in associational life as an outcome, as in the models reported in tables 3.8.A–3.8.E of the online appendix, regression analysis yields results that are closely aligned with expectations from the comparative literature. On the one hand, as for the case of political interest, we find that participatory conceptions of democracy are associated with higher levels of engagement in civic associationism, as coefficients for the participatory index

---

[24] In the six questions we use to calculate this index, not being a member of a certain organization is coded as 0, being a non-active member as 1, and being an active member as 2.

[25] For Indonesia, 85.4% survey vs. 82% recorded in 2019; Malaysia, 80% survey vs. 82.3% in 2018; the Philippines, 81.9% survey vs. 75% in 2019 (midterm elections); Singapore, 88.5% survey vs. 95% in 2020; Thailand, 81% survey vs. 75% in 2019.

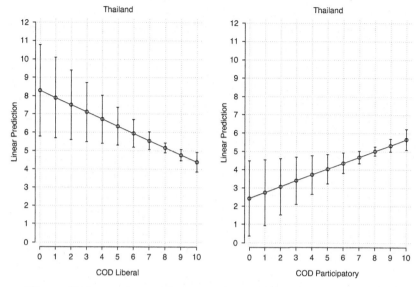

Figure 12 Conceptions of democracy and participation in associations
(Thailand)

are positive and significant in all countries. On the other hand, however, conceptions of democracy can also have a negative impact on participation in civic associations. The estimated coefficient for liberal conceptions of democracy is negatively signed and significant at the .05 level in all countries except Indonesia, which indicates that individuals who understand democracy in liberal terms are significantly less likely to participate in associational life. This negative association is prominent in the case of Thailand, which is represented in Figure 12. The two curves represent the sharply divergent association between two conceptions of democracy – liberal and participatory – and participation in associational life. Whereas higher levels of engagement are predicted for higher levels of participatory understanding of democracy, an inverse relationship is observed for liberal conceptions. For example, a highly liberal democrat (10) is predicted to score almost 4 points lower on our measure of civic engagement (on a 0–12 scale) compared with someone with the lowest levels of liberal democracy understanding. This finding may appear surprising, given that participation in civil society is often associated with liberal ideals, but the negative connection between liberal ideals and informal participation resonates with previous research based on other empirical contexts, some of which is mentioned above. In terms of drivers of informal participation, especially with reference to participation in voluntary associations, Southeast Asian citizens therefore resemble their counterparts in other world regions.

Finally, we estimate a series of logit models, reported in tables 3.9.A–3.9.E of the online appendix, with our binary indicator of turnout at the last general elections as a dependent variable. As the results show, no systematic relationship is observed between any of the three conceptions of democracy and self-reported voting, as the estimated coefficients for the various indexes of conceptions of democracy are almost never statistically significant at conventional levels. We thus see a strong connection between conceptions of democracy and informal participation, but not between democratic ideals and formal participation. To a certain extent, the null finding regarding electoral participation is not surprising. Because we have conceptualized elections as a necessary condition for democracy, we should expect that liberal, egalitarian and participatory democrats alike may share a common belief in the importance of elections. Nevertheless, given the limitation of our indicator of electoral participation, which is based on respondent recall, this finding should be cross-validated in further research.

4.4 Robustness Checks

Our conceptual framework considers democracy as multidimensional. We have assumed that all types of democrats – liberal, egalitarian and participatory – attribute substantial importance to elections, and we have developed twenty distinct items and classified them into four scales with five items each to measure the various dimensions of democracy. The five items on the electoral dimension cover the minimal democratic procedural characteristics focusing on electoral integrity and universal suffrage. The five items on the liberal dimension gather elements regarding individual freedoms and institutional checks and balances. On the participatory dimension, the five items address different elements of political participation. Last, the five egalitarian items cover aspects such as social insurance and inequality. In Section 4.3, we have assessed how each of these dimensions relates to fundamental features of political attitudes and behaviour.

The classification of the items into the dimensions we have followed presents two characteristics. First, we have opted for a balanced approach in which each of the respective dimensions is composed of five items. By providing the same number of items for each dimension to respondents, we are not prioritizing any specific dimension of democracy over the others, and we allow citizens to express their preferences freely rather than indirectly cuing them into some dimensions. Second, we have uniquely classified each item into one exclusive dimension. This approach is sensible as each dimension of democracy can be understood as a Weberian ideal type, which allows us to assess the degree of support and the implications of each dimension.

While we believe that the criteria we followed for our classification of the items are analytically sound, we can probe if alternative item classifications may change our findings to ascertain the robustness of our results. Specifically, it could be argued that not all democracy dimensions are composed by the same number of items, or that some items that we classify into one dimension could be classified into another. In this section we thus examine how alternative operationalizations affect the stability of our results.

We propose three alternative item classifications that may have significant consequences for data analysis, and we will call these robustness checks RC1, RC2 and RC3. In RC1 and RC2 we classify items into different democracy dimensions. RC1 proposes three changes, by reclassifying the following participatory dimension items into the liberal, electoral and egalitarian dimensions, respectively: *People are free to discuss politics in public, demonstrate and protest; Opposition parties are free to operate, criticize the government and run for elections; Women participate in politics as much as men do.* RC1 therefore implies that the participatory dimension only keeps two items. RC2 goes a significant step further than RC1 by considering RC1 changes and also shifting the classification of the following liberal items into the egalitarian category: *Citizens have the same rights regardless of their race and ethnicity* and *Men and women have equal rights.* RC2 also changes the originally egalitarian item that *The government ensures law and order for all* into the liberal category. In RC2, the egalitarian dimension is composed by seven items. Finally, RC3 takes what could be called a lowest common denominator approach in which, rather than opt for alternative classifications, as RC1 or RC2, we exclude the previous items that were reclassified for RC1 and RC2. The main implications on RC3 are not only that each dimension is unbalanced, as in RC1 and RC2, but also only includes 14 items of the 20 available when understanding the respective democratic dimensions. In terms of explanatory power, RC3 has an advantage as it leaves out items that may be sources of dispute, since it only considers items that fit into a clear dimension. However, RC3 has the disadvantage of dropping six individual items as well as losing information.

As can be inferred, by relying on such different operationalizations of all the items in the composition of the democracy dimensions, we follow a conservative approach, as our robustness checks are very demanding. Therefore, if results will be aligned to those we have discussed so far despite the substantial changes that we have described for RC1, RC2 and RC3, this will be a strong indication of the reliability of our results.

We now compare the RCs with the original models. We first studied whether and how the different dimensions of democracy affected the level of satisfaction of democracy. Our main findings here, in accordance with our expectations, were that egalitarian democrats show higher levels of satisfaction with democracy than liberal democrats (i.e. satisfaction with democracy is negatively linked with liberal, and positively linked with egalitarian conceptions of democracy). For the negative effect of liberal understandings of democracy, the findings are substantially stronger in the robustness checks. Where the coefficients were negative and significant (Indonesia and the Philippines), they remain so in all RCs; in the other three countries, for which the results we discussed in 4.3.1 were weaker, eight of the nine RCs return negative and significant coefficients. For egalitarian conceptions of democracy, 11 of the 15 RCs show positive and significant coefficients, while the remaining 4 coefficients are positive as well. As for the participatory dimension, for which results varied across country, the RCs do not suggest a systematic relationship with satisfaction with democracy either.

When exploring the implications of different dimensions of democracy on trust in public institutions, again we hypothesized, and found, that egalitarian understandings are associated with higher levels of trust. Every single RC we have performed confirms this finding. As for the relationship between institutional trust and liberal or participatory understandings, our findings varied by county. The robustness tests yield equally mixed result and vary by country in a similar way, suggesting that neither of these two dimensions is consistently associated with trust in institutions. It is worth mentioning, however, that the RCs confirm the strong and positive association between participatory conceptions of democracy and trust in Indonesia and further show that a very similar relationship exists in Malaysia.[26] As for trust in the army, the results discussed for the Indonesian vs. the Thai case hold in all RCs for Indonesia, while they are inconsistent for Thailand.

The third section of our analysis has focused into a more diffuse level of support for democracy, a belief of democracy as the most desirable political system and a rejection of its authoritarian alternatives. Although initially we did not outline any strong theoretical expectations, we found that the liberal conception index was positively associated with such diffuse support for democracy in all five countries, while the egalitarian and participatory dimensions behave more erratically. As in the main analysis, all three robustness checks find a positive relationship between the liberal dimension and the diffuse support for democracy, with 15 out of 15 estimated coefficients positively signed. However, the estimated

---

[26] All three RCs for Malaysia have positive and significant coefficients. In the original model, the coefficient was positive but not significant.

coefficients for Thailand and Indonesia, while positive, are not significant at conventional levels. Results from the RCs are similar when we estimate models with our indicator of 'genuine' democratic support, which we did for Singapore and Thailand. Here, the coefficient for liberal understandings of democracy is always positive, and significant in three cases out of six. Finally, the egalitarian and participatory dimensions behave as in the main analysis.

The last part of the analysis has looked at whether and how several democratic dimensions impact the different aspects of political participation. Specifically, we proposed that those with strong participatory conceptions of democracy are more likely to participate in politics, especially through informal channels. In contrast, for liberal democrats, such participation would be less likely to take place through informal avenues. We have assessed such claim with three complementary measures of formal and informal political participation. The first measures interest in politics and the main finding was a strong and consistently positive relation between participatory understandings of democracy and political interest in all countries. Such pattern also holds across all the robustness checks we have run, with the exception of Singapore in RC1, where the sign is positive but not significant. The second measure was self-reported data on membership in various types of civic and political associations. The analysis points at a positive and significant relation between participatory conceptions of democracy and higher levels of engagement in civic associationism. Results from the RCs show the same pattern, with all 15 coefficients positive and significant. The third and final measure gathered formal participation by asking whether respondents had voted in the last general elections. In the original analysis, we did not find any systematic relationship between any of the democracy conceptions assessed and voter turnout. The results of the robustness checks are the same.

To conclude this section, in our aim to assess how Southeast Asian citizens understand democracy, we have first proposed a series of democracy dimensions in which individuals organize their evaluations. Acknowledging that some of the components of the democracy dimensions we have relied upon could be classified differently, we have proceeded with three different robustness checks that offer alternative classifications of the dimensions. Overall, our approach and the alternative classifications yield very similar results, which strengthen our general findings.

5 Conclusions

The idea of democracy today enjoys a broad normative appeal. Politicians in almost all regimes, authoritarian or democratic, embrace some form of democratic rhetoric to legitimize their rule. Ordinary citizens almost everywhere continue to value living in a democracy as something desirable and worth aspiring to. Even leaders who push agendas of autocratization in old and new democracies alike typically justify their actions as being necessary to preserve or deepen democracy, and are careful to maintain a democratic façade to conceal their real intentions (Curato & Fossati, 2020; Glasius, 2018). However, far from suggesting that democracy has consolidated to become 'the only game in town', the apparent normative primacy of democracy is in fact a consensus on a vague concept, and it conceals a high level of contentiousness among democratic ideals. In name, democracy may remain attractive for most political elites and ordinary citizens, but the extreme heterogeneity in how this term is understood by different people in different places means that, to be meaningful, abstract measures of support for democracy must always be qualified and contextualized.

This Element has analysed the various – and potentially conflicting – popular understandings of democracy in Southeast Asia, especially as they pertain to democracy's liberal, egalitarian and participatory dimensions. We have started with the premise that democracy is a complex, multifaceted construct. To the extent to which ordinary citizens understand this concept and its multidimensionality, we must acknowledge that they will disagree about what democracy, exactly, is about. This diversity and contentiousness results, first, from the different political–historical trajectories that have shaped democratic development in each country. Democracy may be universally desirable, but what it means when people say that they support democracy is highly contingent on the specificities of a certain political context, in which leaders have used their positions of power to shape the discourse on democracy according to their own interests.

Second, as with any lofty ideal, what is meant by 'democracy' varies across individuals within any population. The 'D-word' is often vague enough and contentious enough that democracy, in a way, may be 'in the eye of the beholder', as everyone can project their own normative orientations onto this concept. An important implication of this reality is that research on democratic attitudes must take popular understandings of democracy seriously, analysing the complexity of their structure, how priorities and values vary across social groups and countries, and what the implications are of holding different views of democracy for other attitudes and political behaviour.

The empirical realm where we have chosen to investigate these questions is that of Southeast Asia, a region of remarkable diversity. We have selected five countries that exhibit substantially different trajectories of democratic development and current levels of democracy. Indonesia is the most democratic in the group, and is a case in which democracy has survived for two decades despite high levels of ethno-religious fractionalization, corruption and economic inequality. At the opposite end of the spectrum, Thailand is a country where democratic politics have been largely suspended since 2014, when a military coup supported by an illiberal monarchy replaced a democratically elected government. In between these two extremes, our cases range from the Philippines, where recent years have witnessed a substantial erosion of democracy, to Malaysia and Singapore, two illiberal regimes that have shown high levels of political stability over the last few decades. This empirical focus puts us in a strong position to contribute to a body of literature in which studies of established Western democracies dominate, as we include countries that differ markedly from Western cases in their political cultures and historical legacies. At the same time, we adopt a conceptual framework developed from the theoretical and comparative literature on democratic attitudes to ensure that our analysis is in conversation with existing research.

Our first set of findings pertain to the structure of conceptions of democracy among Southeast Asian publics. As we expected, we found that Southeast Asians hold complex and multidimensional conceptions of democracy, as people in other world regions do. Our questionnaire presented survey participants with an exhaustive, yet easy-to-understand, list of various features that could be considered essential for democracy, and respondents were given the freedom to rate each of these items independently. Responses to these questions show that most participants attributed very high levels of importance to both liberal and egalitarian elements of democracy; other participants also highly valued participatory elements. When surveys ask citizens open questions about the meaning of democracy, most respondents are unable to describe more than one feature. However, when their task as respondents is assisted with prompts that suggest various democratic ideas, a more complex picture emerges. In Southeast Asia, as elsewhere, different notions of democracy resonate and co-exist among mass publics.

Against this background, a recurring debate in the Southeast Asia–based literature is what conception of democracy, if any, is predominant in the region. Do Southeast Asians understand democracy primarily in terms of individual rights and liberties, or do they see democracy primarily as a matter of policy outcomes that benefit most of the population? Our analysis suggests that this question may miss the mark, as these two dimensions of democracy – liberal and egalitarian – are both highly correlated and considered to be equally essential features of democracy.

Among the thousands of people we have interviewed, there is a clear awareness that democracy, beyond free and fair elections, is primarily a matter of individual freedoms, civil liberties and equal rights for all. At the same time, however, there is an equally strong perception that addressing social inequalities and providing basic services to all are also essential features of democratic politics. From a conceptual standpoint, the two dimensions are of course distinct, and there is a tension between the two that at times may be difficult to resolve. But in practice, liberal and egalitarian values can be compatible, and they certainly seem to be closely intertwined in the minds of the Southeast Asian publics we have studied. This is an especially interesting finding against the background of political development in the region, where, as we have discussed in the historical introductions in Section 2, liberal ideas of democracy have typically been rather marginal. Further research, instead of seeking to establish which of the two dimensions is predominant, could acknowledge that both dimensions are strongly rooted in public opinion in this region, and explore the conditions under which a certain conception may be prioritized over others.

Although the dichotomy between liberal and social–egalitarian values should be reconsidered, our results do point to a certain duality in the structure of the meaning of democracy in Southeast Asia. Along with the dominant idea of democracy – which blends liberal and egalitarian items – a distinct, participatory understanding of democracy is also present in all countries. As we discussed, participatory values are not as broadly endorsed as liberal or social–egalitarian ones, but nevertheless we find in our empirical analysis that participatory democracy is a concept that resonates among Southeast Asian publics – in certain social segments, quite strongly. Perhaps most importantly, we have found that participatory understandings of democracy are frequently and significantly connected with important attitudinal and behavioural outcomes in all countries, and sometimes in ways that are quite different from liberal notions of democracy. Participatory ideas of democracy are therefore a crucial, if minoritarian, strand of the meaning of democracy as conceptualized by ordinary people in Southeast Asia. Given that most of the current survey-based research on democratic attitudes in the region overlooks this dimension entirely, we consider our recognition of the role of participatory democratic ideals to be an especially important contribution of this Element.

Our analysis of socio-demographic drivers of different conceptions of democracy also offers some interesting insights. Perhaps in the context of the diverse societies of Southeast Asia, the most interesting findings concern the link between conceptions of democracy and social identities such as religion and ethnicity. In Indonesia, where politics features a cultural–religious cleavage as the main axis of ideological competition, religion is a predictor of individual-level views of democracy, as Muslims are less likely to appreciate liberal elements as being essential for democracy. A similar picture emerges in

Malaysia, where the dominant Malays tend to be more social–egalitarian in their democratic ideals, whereas the largest ethnic minority, the Chinese, are more liberal. These findings are an apt illustration of the close connection between historical legacies (colonial and post-colonial) and public understandings of democracy. Differences across ethnic and religious groups in cultural and normative values, which result from historical patterns of inter-ethnic relations and state formation, are reflected in divergent understandings of democracy across ethno-religious groups.

We have also found strong evidence that public understandings of democracy shape how people evaluate democratic performance. We have analysed a range of indicators as measures of public satisfaction with democratic practice in the five countries, and despite some important differences across countries, we have identified a common pattern. Whereas those who understand democracy in egalitarian terms tend to be more satisfied with democracy, liberal democrats and participatory democrats are more critical in evaluating the performance of democratic institutions.

This is an important finding that shows an intimate connection between popular understandings of democracy and patterns of democratic legitimacy in the region. When Southeast Asian political regimes are evaluated based on their ability to provide public goods and address social and economic issues, they tend to receive fairly high levels of popular support. In contrast, when they are evaluated on their performance in fostering liberal values and civil liberties, their scorecard is more negative. As we have discussed, these findings resonate with the fact that democracy in Southeast Asia has generally performed better in the social–egalitarian domain than in implementing liberal and participatory principles, to the extent that none of the five countries we study is usually considered as a liberal democracy. There is, therefore, a latent demand for liberalism and participatory politics in Southeast Asia that has yet to be satisfied by the region's political regimes. The legitimacy of these regimes, thus, appears to rest primarily on their ability to ensure adequate levels of social and economic progress. Although this is a testament to the important results that have been achieved in this area, it is also a liability in that it exposes such regimes to the risk of severe legitimacy crises that may arise, should they become less able to deliver such desirable social–economic outcomes.

However, the differences in evaluations of democratic performance and institutional trust between egalitarian democrats on the one hand, and liberal–participatory democrats on the other, do not extend to more generalized support for democracy as a political regime. Here, what we find is that support for democracy is positively and significantly associated with *liberal* ideas of democracy. It is, therefore, liberal democrats who are the most supportive of democracy as a political regime, which is an interesting finding against the background (highlighted above) of the high level of semantic confusion that often surrounds the word 'democracy'. Despite such ambiguity, the clear connection between liberal understandings of democracy and support for democracy indicates that there is a type of democrat who is more committed to democracy than others, and that this group sees democracy as a matter of individual rights and checks and balances to constrain the power of the executive. Perhaps this strong association exists because democracy is needed to enforce this sort of liberal values, whereas to a certain degree, participatory and egalitarian aspirations can be realized in non-democratic regimes as well. Liberal democrats can therefore be considered an especially important ideological group in terms of the role citizens must play in defending democracy, because their normative affinity for liberalism makes them especially supportive of democratic constitutional arrangements.

References

Anderson, B. (1988). Cacique democracy and the Philippines: Origins and dreams. *New Left Review*, (169), *1*(3), 3–33.

Ariely, G. (2013). Public administration and citizen satisfaction with democracy: Cross-national evidence. *International Review of Administrative Sciences*, *79*(4), 747–66.

Aspinall, E. (2005). *Opposing Suharto: Compromise, resistance, and regime change in Indonesia*. Stanford University Press.

Aspinall, E., Fossati, D., Muhtadi, B., & Warburton, E. (2020). Elite, masses and democratic decline in Indonesia. *Democratisation*, *27*(4), 505–26.

Baker, R., Brick, J. M., Bates, N. A. et al. (2013). Summary report of the AAPOR task force on non-probability sampling. *Journal of Survey Statistics and Methodology*, *1*(2), 90–143.

Baniamin, H. M. (2020). Citizens' inflated perceptions of the extent of democracy in different African countries: Are individuals' notions of the state an answer to the puzzle? *Zeitschrift für Vergleichende Politikwissenschaft*, *14*(4), 321–43.

Barber, B. (2003). *Strong democracy: Participatory politics for a new age*. University of California Press.

Barr, M. D. (2019). *Singapore: A modern history*. IB Tauris.

Baviskar, S., & Malone, M. F. (2004). What democracy means to citizens – and why it matters. *European Review of Latin American and Caribbean Studies*, *76*(2), 3–23.

Bengtsson, Å., & Christensen, H. (2016). Ideals and actions: Do citizens' patterns of political participation correspond to their conceptions of democracy? *Government and Opposition*, *51*(2), 234–60.

Berinsky, A. J., Huber, G. A., & Lenz, G. S. (2012). Evaluating online labor markets for experimental research: Amazon. com's Mechanical Turk. *Political Analysis*, *20*(3), 351–68.

Bermeo, N. (2016). On democratic backsliding. *Journal of Democracy*, *27*(1), 5–19.

Bourchier, D. (2014). *Illiberal democracy in Indonesia: The ideology of the family state*. Routledge.

Brady, H. E., Verba, S., & Schlozman, K. L. (1995). Beyond SES: A resource model of political participation. *American Political Science Review*, *89*(2), 271–94.

Bratton, M., Mattes, R., & Gyimah-Boadi, E. (2005). *Public opinion, democracy, and market reform in Africa*. Cambridge University Press.

Camp, R. A. (2001). *Citizen views of democracy in Latin America*. University of Pittsburgh Press.

Canache, D. (2012). Citizens' conceptualizations of democracy: Structural complexity, substantive content, and political significance. *Comparative Political Studies*, *45*(9), 1132–58.

Canache, D., Mondak, J. J., & Seligson, M. A. (2001). Meaning and measurement in cross-national research on satisfaction with democracy. *Public Opinion Quarterly*, *65*(4), 506–28.

Case, W. (2013). *Politics in Southeast Asia: Democracy or less*. Routledge.

Ceka, B., & Magalhaes, P. C. (2020). Do the rich and the poor have different conceptions of democracy? Socioeconomic status, inequality, and the political status quo. *Comparative Politics*, *52*(3), 383–412.

Chambers, P., & Waitoolkiat, N. (2016). The resilience of monarchised military in Thailand. *Journal of Contemporary Asia*, *46*(3), 425–44.

Cho, Y. (2014). To know democracy is to love it: A cross-national analysis of democratic understanding and political support for democracy. *Political Research Quarterly*, *67*(3), 478–88.

Chu, Y.- h., Diamond, L., Nathan, A. J., & Shin, D. C. (2008). *How East Asians view democracy*. Columbia University Press.

Chu, Y.- h., & Huang, M.- h. (2010). The meanings of democracy: Solving an Asian puzzle. *Journal of Democracy*, *21*(4), 114–22.

Chua, B.-H. (1997). *Communitarian ideology and democracy in Singapore* (Vol. 9). Psychology Press.

Claassen, C. (2020). Does public support help democracy survive? *American Journal of Political Science*, *64*(1), 118–34.

Clarke, G. (2006). *The politics of NGOs in Southeast Asia: Participation and protest in the Philippines*. Routledge.

Clifford, S., Jewell, R. M., & Waggoner, P. D. (2015). Are samples drawn from Mechanical Turk valid for research on political ideology? *Research & Politics*, *2*(4), 2053168015622072.

Cohen, J. (1997). Procedure and substance in deliberative democracy. In J. Bohman & W. Rehg (Eds.), *Deliberative democracy: Essays on reason and politics* (pp. 407–38). MIT Press.

Collier, D., & Levitsky, S. (1997). Democracy with adjectives: Conceptual innovation in comparative research. *World Politics*, *49*(3), 430–51.

Connors, M. (2007). *Democracy and national identity in Thailand* (Vol. 2). NIAS Press.

Connors, M. (2016). Political ideologies and liberalism in Southeast Asia: A review article. *Asian Review*, *29*(2), 101–14.

Coppedge, M., Gerring, J., Altman, D. et al. (2011). Conceptualizing and measuring democracy: A new approach. *Perspectives on Politics*, *9*(2) 247–67.

Cordero, G., & Simón, P. (2016). Economic crisis and support for democracy in Europe. *West European Politics*, *39*(2), 305–25.

Curato, N., & Fossati, D. (2020). Authoritarian innovations. *Democratisation*, *27*(6), 1006–20.

Dahl, R. A. (1973). *Polyarchy: Participation and opposition*. Yale University Press.

Dalton, R. J. (1994). Communists and democrats: Democratic attitudes in the two Germanies. *British Journal of Political Science*, *24*(4), 469–93.

Dalton, R. J., Sin, T.-c., & Jou, W. (2007). Understanding democracy: Data from unlikely places. *Journal of Democracy*, *18*(4), 142–56.

David, R., & Holliday, I. (2018). *Liberalism and democracy in Myanmar*. Oxford University Press.

Dettman, S. (2020). Authoritarian innovations and democratic reform in the 'New Malaysia'. *Democratization*, *27*(6), 1037–52.

Diamond, L. (1992). Promoting democracy. *Foreign Policy*, (87), 25–46.

Diamond, L. (1999). *Developing democracy: Toward consolidation*. Johns Hopkins University Press.

Diamond, L. (2002). Elections without democracy: Thinking about hybrid regimes. *Journal of Democracy*, *13*(2), 21–35.

Dore, G., Ku, J. H., & Jackson, K. (2014). *Incomplete democracies in the Asia-Pacific: Evidence from Indonesia, Korea, the Philippines and Thailand*. Springer.

Easton, D. (1975). A re-assessment of the concept of political support. *British Journal of Political Science*, *5*(4), 435–57.

Fawcett, E. (2018). *Liberalism: The life of an idea*. Princeton University Press.

Feith, H. (1962). *The decline of constitutional democracy in Indonesia*. Cornell University Press.

Feldman, K. A., & Newcomb, T. M. (2020). *The impact of college on students*. Routledge.

Fernandez, K. E., & Kuenzi, M. (2010). Crime and support for democracy in Africa and Latin America. *Political Studies*, *58*(3), 450–71.

Ferrara, F. (2015). *The political development of modern Thailand*. Cambridge University Press.

Ferrín, M., & Kriesi, H. (2016). *How Europeans view and evaluate democracy*. Oxford University Press.

Fish, M. S. (2002). Islam and authoritarianism. *World Politics*, *55*(1), 4–37.

Fishkin, J. S. (1991). *Democracy and deliberation: New directions for democratic reform*. Yale University Press.

Fossati, D. (2019). The resurgence of ideology in Indonesia: Political Islam, aliran and political behavior. *Journal of Current Southeast Asian Affairs*, *38*(2), 119–48.

Fossati, D. (2022). *Unity through division: Political Islam, representation and democracy in Indonesia*. Cambridge University Press.

Fossati, D., & Martinez i Coma, F. (2020). How popular conceptions of democracy shape democratic support in Indonesia. In T. Power & E. Warburton (Eds.), *Democracy in Indonesia: From stagnation to regression?* (pp. 166–88). ISEAS.

Fossati, D., Muhtadi, B., & Warburton, E. (2022). Why democrats abandon democracy: Evidence from four survey experiments. *Party Politics*, *28*(3), 554–66.

Gandhi, J., & Lust-Okar, E. (2009). Elections under authoritarianism. *Annual Review of Political Science*, *12*, 403–22.

Gherghina, S., & Geissel, B. (2017). Linking democratic preferences and political participation: Evidence from Germany. *Political Studies*, *65* (1_suppl), 24–42.

Giersdorf, S., & Croissant, A. (2011). Civil society and competitive authoritarianism in Malaysia. *Journal of Civil Society*, *7*(1), 1–21.

Gilley, B. (2006). The determinants of state legitimacy: Results for 72 countries. *International Political Science Review*, *27*(1), 47–71.

Glasius, M. (2018). What authoritarianism is . . . and is not: A practice perspective. *International Affairs*, *94*(3), 515–33.

Graham, M., & Svolik, M. W. (2020). Democracy in America? Partisanship, polarization, and the robustness of support for democracy in the United States. *American Political Science Review*, *114*(2), 392–409.

Haggard, S., & Kaufman, R. (2021). *Backsliding: Democratic regress in the contemporary world*. Cambridge University Press.

Hamid, S. (2014). *Temptations of power: Islamists and illiberal democracy in a new Middle East*. Oxford University Press.

Harapan, H., Wagner, A. L., Yufika, A. et al. (2020). Acceptance of a COVID-19 vaccine in Southeast Asia: A cross-sectional study in Indonesia. *Frontiers in Public Health*, *8*.

Hassan, S., & Weiss, M. (2012). *Social movement Malaysia*. Routledge.

Helmke, G., & Levitsky, S. (2006). *Informal institutions and democracy: Lessons from Latin America*. Johns Hopkins University Press.

Hewison, K. (1997). The monarchy and democratisation. In Kevin Hewison (Ed.), *Political change in Thailand* (pp. 58–74). Routledge.

Hewison, K. (2012). Class, Inequality and Politics. In M. Montesano, Pavin Chachavalpongpun & Aekapol Chongvilaivan (Eds.), *Perspectives on a Divided Thailand, Singapore:* Institute of South East Asian Studies (pp. - 143–60).

Ho, K. L. (2003). *Shared responsibilities, unshared power: The politics of policy-making in Singapore*. Marshall Cavendish International.

Hooghe, M., Marien, S., & Oser, J. (2017). Great expectations: The effect of democratic ideals on political trust in European democracies. *Contemporary Politics, 23*(2), 214–30.

Howard, M. M., & Gilbert, L. (2008). A cross-national comparison of the internal effects of participation in voluntary organizations. *Political Studies, 56*(1), 12–32.

Huang, M.- h. (2017). Cognitive involvement and democratic understanding. In T.-j. Cheng & Y.-h. Chu (Eds.), *Routledge handbook of democratization in East Asia* (pp. 297–313). Routledge.

Huang, M.- h., Chang, Y.- t., & Chu, Y.- h. (2008). Identifying sources of democratic legitimacy: A multilevel analysis. *Electoral Studies, 27*(1), 45–62.

Huang, M.-H., Chu, Y.-h., & Chang, Y.-t. (2013). Popular understandings of democracy and regime legitimacy in East Asia. *Taiwan Journal of Democracy, 9*(1), 147–71.

Huber, E., Rueschemeyer, D., & Stephens, J. D. (1997). The paradoxes of contemporary democracy: Formal, participatory, and social dimensions. *Comparative Politics, 29*(3), 323–42.

Inglehart, R. (1997). *Modernization and postmodernization: Cultural, economic, and political change in 43 societies*. Princeton University Press.

Inglehart, R. (2003). How solid is mass support for democracy – and how can we measure it? *PS: Political Science & Politics, 36*(1), 51–7.

Jayasuriya, K., & Rodan, G. (2007). Beyond hybrid regimes: More participation, less contestation in Southeast Asia. *Democratization, 14*(5), 773–94.

King, D. Y. (2003). *Half-hearted reform: Electoral institutions and the struggle for democracy in Indonesia*. Greenwood Publishing Group.

Kirsch, H., & Welzel, C. (2019). Democracy misunderstood: Authoritarian notions of democracy around the globe. *Social Forces, 98*(1), 59–92.

Kriesi, H. (2018). The implications of the euro crisis for democracy. *Journal of European Public Policy, 25*(1), 59–82.

Laffan, M. F. (2003). *Islamic nationhood and colonial Indonesia: The umma below the winds*. Routledge.

Lai, L. (2019, October 1). Tommy Koh laments that Singapore is a First World country with Third World citizens. *The Strait Times*.

Lechler, M., & Sunde, U. (2019). Individual life horizon influences attitudes toward democracy. *American Political Science Review, 113*(3), 860–7.

Letsa, N. W., & Wilfahrt, M. (2018). Popular support for democracy in autocratic regimes: A micro-level analysis of preferences. *Comparative Politics*, *50*(2), 231–73.

Lijphart, A. (1969). Consociational democracy. *World Politics*, *21*(2), 207–25.

Lindberg, S. I., Coppedge, M., Gerring, J., & Teorell, J. (2014). V-Dem: A new way to measure democracy. *Journal of Democracy*, *25*(3), 159–69.

Linz, J. J., & Stepan, A. (1996). *Problems of democratic transition and consolidation: Southern Europe, South America, and post-communist Europe*. Johns Hopkins University Press.

Lipset, S. M. (1959). Some social requisites of democracy: Economic development and political legitimacy. *American Political Science Review*, *53*(1), 69–105.

Lührmann, A., & Lindberg, S. I. (2019). A third wave of autocratization is here: What is new about it? *Democratization*, *27*(7), 1095–113.

Lussier, D. N., & Fish, M. S. (2012). Indonesia: The benefits of civic engagement. *Journal of Democracy*, *23*(1), 70–84.

Magalhães, P. C. (2014). Government effectiveness and support for democracy. *European Journal of Political Research*, *53*(1), 77–97.

Magalhães, P. C. (2016). Economic evaluations, procedural fairness, and satisfaction with democracy. *Political Research Quarterly*, *69*(3), 522–34.

Mattes, R., & Bratton, M. (2007). Learning about democracy in Africa: Awareness, performance, and experience. *American Journal of Political Science*, *51*(1), 192–217.

Mauzy, D. (2013). Malaysia: Malay political hegemony and 'coercive consociationalism'. In J. McGarry and B. O'Leary (Eds.), *The politics of ethnic conflict regulation* (pp. 118–39). Routledge.

Maxwell, S. R. (2019). Perceived threat of crime, authoritarianism, and the rise of a populist president in the Philippines. *International Journal of Comparative and Applied Criminal Justice*, *43*(3), 207–18.

May, R., & Selochan, V. (2004). *The military and democracy in Asia and the Pacific*. Australian National University Press.

McCargo, D. (2020). *Fighting for virtue: Justice and politics in Thailand*. Cornell University Press.

Means, G. P. (1996). Soft authoritarianism in Malaysia and Singapore. *Journal of Democracy*, *7*(4), 103–17.

Mietzner, M. (2018). Fighting illiberalism with illiberalism: Islamist populism and democratic deconsolidation in Indonesia. *Pacific Affairs*, *91*(2), 261–82.

Munck, G. L. (2016). What is democracy? A reconceptualization of the quality of democracy. *Democratization*, *23*(1), 1–26.

Munck, G. L., & Verkuilen, J. (2002). Conceptualizing and measuring democracy: Evaluating alternative indices. *Comparative Political Studies, 35*(1), 5–34.

Musolf, L. D., & Springer, J. F. (1979). *Malaysia's parliamentary system: Representative politics and policymaking in a divided society.* Routledge.

Mutalib, H. (2000). Illiberal democracy and the future of opposition in Singapore. *Third World Quarterly, 21*(2), 313–42.

Nadzri, M. M. (2018). The 14th general election, the fall of Barisan Nasional, and political development in Malaysia, 1957–2018. *Journal of Current Southeast Asian Affairs, 37*(3), 139–71.

Norris, P. (2011). *Democratic deficit: Critical citizens revisited.* Cambridge University Press.

Norris, P. (2017). The conceptual framework of political support. In S. Zmerli and T. W.G. van der Meer (Eds.), *Handbook on political trust* (pp. 19–32). Edward Elgar.

Norton, E. (2012). Illiberal democrats versus undemocratic liberals: The struggle over the future of Thailand's fragile democracy. *Asian Journal of Political Science, 20*(1), 46–69.

O'Donnell, G. A. (1994). Delegative democracy. *Journal of Democracy, 5*(1), 55–69.

Ortmann, S. (2015). Political change and civil society coalitions in Singapore. *Government and Opposition, 50*(1), 119–39.

Owen, A. L., Videras, J., & Willemsen, C. (2008). Democracy, participation, and life satisfaction. *Social Science Quarterly, 89*(4), 987–1005.

Pepinsky, T. (2017). Southeast Asia: Voting against disorder. *Journal of Democracy, 28*(2), 120–31.

Power, T., & Warburton, E. (Eds.). (2020). *Democracy in Indonesia: From stagnation to regression?* ISEAS.

Przeworski, A., Alvarez, M., Cheibub, J., & Limongi, F. (2000). *Democracy and development: Political institutions and well-being in the world, 1950–1990.* Cambridge University Press.

Radcliff, B., & Shufeldt, G. (2016). Direct democracy and subjective well-being: The initiative and life satisfaction in the American states. *Social Indicators Research, 128*(3), 1405–23.

Reilly, B. (2017). An elephant's graveyard? Democracy and development in East Asia. *Government and Opposition, 52*(1), 162–83.

Robbins, M. (2015). After the Arab Spring: People still want democracy. *Journal of Democracy, 26*(4), 80–9.

Rodan, G. (2018). *Participation without democracy: Containing conflict in Southeast Asia.* Cornell University Press.

Rohrschneider, R. (2002). The democracy deficit and mass support for an EU-wide government. *American Journal of Political Science, 46*(2), 463–75.

Schedler, A., & Sarsfield, R. (2007). Democrats with adjectives: Linking direct and indirect measures of democratic support. *European Journal of Political Research, 46*(5), 637–59.

Schumpeter, J. A. (1942). *Capitalism, socialism and democracy.* Routledge.

Seligson, M. A. (2004). The political culture of democracy in Mexico, Central America and Colombia, 2004. *Nashville, Latin American Public Opinion Project-United States Agency for International Development, 236,* 1–133.

Shin, D. C., & Kim, H. J. (2018). How global citizenries think about democracy: An evaluation and synthesis of recent public opinion research. *Japanese Journal of Political Science, 19*(2), 222–49.

Singer, M. M. (2011). Who says 'It's the economy'? Cross-national and cross-individual variation in the salience of economic performance. *Comparative Political Studies, 44*(3), 284–312.

Sinpeng, A. (2017). Participatory inequality in online and offline political engagement in Thailand. *Pacific Affairs, 90*(2), 253–74.

Sinpeng, A. (2021). *Opposing democracy in the digital age: The yellow shirts in Thailand.* University of Michigan Press.

Slater, D. (2013). Democratic careening. *World Politics, 65*(4), 729–63.

Sombatpoonsiri, J. (2021). *A struggle for democracy in divided Thailand.* Working Paper. Institute of Asian Studies, Chulalongkorn University.

Teehankee, J. C. (2012). Clientelism and party politics in the Philippines. In D. Tomsa and A. Ufen (Eds.), *Party politics in Southeast Asia* (pp. 204–32). Routledge.

Tejapira, K. (2016). The irony of democratization and the decline of royal hegemony in Thailand. *Southeast Asian Studies, 5*(2), 219–37.

Tessler, M., Jamal, A., & Robbins, M. (2012). New findings on Arabs and democracy. *Journal of Democracy, 23*(4), 89–103.

Thomassen, J., Andeweg, R., & Van Ham, C. (2017). Political trust and the decline of legitimacy debate: A theoretical and empirical investigation into their interrelationship. In S. Zmerli and T. W.G. van der Meer (Eds.), *Handbook on political trust* (pp.509–25). Edward Elgar.

Thompson, M. R. (2016). Bloodied democracy: Duterte and the death of liberal reformism in the Philippines. *Journal of Current Southeast Asian Affairs, 35*(3), 39–68.

Thompson, M. R. (2021). The paradoxes of 'vernacularised' liberalism in Southeast Asia. *Asian Studies Review,* 1–20. http://DOI:10.1080/10357823.2021.1940842.

Thum, P. (2013). *'The fundamental issue is anti-colonialism, not merger':* *Singapore's 'progressive left', operation coldstore, and the creation of* *Malaysia.* Asia Research Institute, Working Paper Series No.211.

Ulbricht, T. (2018). Perceptions and conceptions of democracy: Applying thick concepts of democracy to reassess desires for democracy. *Comparative Political Studies, 51*(11), 1387–440.

Van de Walle, S., & Bouckaert, G. (2003). Public service performance and trust in government: The problem of causality. *International Journal of Public Administration, 26*(8–9), 891–913.

Vickers, A. (2013). *A history of modern Indonesia.* Cambridge University Press.

Wang, Z. (2007). Public support for democracy in China. *Journal of Contemporary China, 16*(53), 561–79.

Weiss, M. L. (2006). *Protest and possibilities: Civil society and coalitions for political change in Malaysia.* Stanford University Press.

Weiss, M. L. (2021). Paradoxes of reform: Protest, progress and polarization in Malaysia. In N. Stoltzfus and C. Osmar (Eds.), *The power of populism and people: Resistance and protest in the modern world* (p. 115–36). Bloomsbury.

Welzel, C. (2013). *Freedom rising.* Cambridge University Press.

Welzel, C. (2021). Why the future is democratic. *Journal of Democracy, 32*(2), 132–44.

Welzel, C., & Inglehart, R. (2008). The role of ordinary people in democratization. *Journal of Democracy, 19*(1), 126–40.

Young, I. M. (2002). *Inclusion and democracy.* Oxford University Press.

Zakaria, F. (2007). *The future of freedom: Illiberal democracy at home and abroad* (Revised ed.). WW Norton.

Zakaria, F., & Yew, L. K. (1994). Culture is destiny: A conversation with Lee Kuan Yew. *Foreign Affairs, 73*(2), 109–27.

Zhai, Y. (2019). Popular conceptions of democracy and democratic satisfaction in China. *International Political Science Review, 40*(2), 246–62.

Acknowledgements

We are thankful for financial support from the Australian Research Council, as data collection for this research was funded through a Discovery Project Grant awarded to Ferran Martinez i Coma [Grant Number: DP190101978]. This project was also supported by Hong Kong's University Grant Council's Early Career Scheme (ECS) Grant 21603520 awarded to Diego Fossati. We are grateful to Brinda Mehra for research assistance on Section 2.2.

We would also like to express our deep gratitude to our wives, Junxiu and María Cayetana, for their love and support. This Element is for them.

To Junxiu
To María Cayetana

Politics and Society in Southeast Asia

Edward Aspinall

Australian National University

Edward Aspinall is a professor of politics at the Coral Bell School of Asia-Pacific Affairs, Australian National University. A specialist of Southeast Asia, especially Indonesia, much of his research has focused on democratisation, ethnic politics and civil society in Indonesia and, most recently, clientelism across Southeast Asia.

Meredith L. Weiss

University at Albany, SUNY

Meredith L. Weiss is Professor of Political Science at the University at Albany, SUNY. Her research addresses political mobilization and contention, the politics of identity and development, and electoral politics in Southeast Asia, with particular focus on Malaysia and Singapore.

About the Series

The Elements series Politics and Society in Southeast Asia includes both country-specific and thematic studies on one of the world's most dynamic regions. Each title, written by a leading scholar of that country or theme, combines a succinct, comprehensive, up-to-date overview of debates in the scholarly literature with original analysis and a clear argument.

Cambridge Elements ≡

Politics and Society in Southeast Asia

Printed in the United States
by Baker & Taylor Publisher Services